Economics Island

Table of Contents

I. Introduction..5

II. Economics Island..11

    The Barter System, Comparative Advantage, and Currency..12

    Currency...17

    Monopoly and Competition........................22

    Input Costs..24

    Opportunity Costs.....................................25

    Monopoly..28

    Supply and Demand.................................33

    Leisure Time and Innovation......................39

    The Stock Market....................................43

    Interest Rates and the Price of Money...........47

    Monetary Policy and the Supply and Demand of Money..50

    International Trade....................................52

    Currency and Exchange Rates.....................55

III. The Problem with Economic Indicators..............63

    Gross Domestic Product (GDP)...................68

    The Stock Market; as an indicator................75

    Housing Market......................................82

The Unemployment Rate............................103

The Perfect Society................................113

Productivity...115

Efficiency...126

Trade Surplus.......................................132

IV. Growing the Pie.....................................111

V. Conclusion...147

I. Introduction

Interest in economics, as both an academic pursuit and a topic for casual conversation, has increased greatly in recent years. This increase is based on the utilization of economic reasoning in various academic genres and a growing concern for pocketbook issues and their perceived connection to the general field of economics. The past arguments dealing with different economic systems have largely ended in this country, due mainly to the success of the current capitalist system. These debates still occur in the academic setting along with arguments over economic thought; currently centering on Keynesian v. Monetarist thinking. However, most individuals, when talking about economics, focus on government policy; what will taxes be, how much government will spend, or what will the distribution of funds be. Individuals and "experts" also focus on the health of the economy. The economy is usually described as either strong or weak, up or down. The problem many casual economic observers, and even many non-casual observers, have is that they confuse two core ideas underlying the economy. It is important to remember that how the economic pie is distributed is a totally different concept than how the total economic pie is increased. A common symbol used to explain economic theory is the pie. The pie represents the goods and services in the economy; the bigger the pie gets, the more there is to eat. Similarly the larger the economy gets, the more goods and services there are for society to enjoy. Once this point is made clear, it is easier to understand the ways in which the economy can be strengthened. The ways in which the economy is strengthened and what this actually means is the focus of this book. A clear representation of these, along with a simple explanation of basic economic concepts, free of complicated technical jargon, are the goals this author hopes to achieve.

The book will be broken down into three sections; first, an explanation of basic ideas using the fictional motif of Economics Island, second a criticism of current economic indicators, and finally an introduction of new economic indicators based on a proper understanding of economic growth. The purpose of the book is threefold. The first is to create within the reader an understanding of some basic economic principles.

These principles are advanced through the teaching tool of the island as a way to make the concepts less technical and more tangible. Part of the rationale for using this method is the difficulty most casual readers have with complicated economic terms and remote examples. The other reason is that by developing the concepts from the ground up, the reader is able to move away from the common misconceptions that are associated with economic concepts when dealing with the present-day system. This last point will make more sense as the book progresses.

The second goal of the book is to lay out a critique of the current economic indicators. These indicators are common measurements and statistics used to evaluate the strength or weakness of the economy. The chosen indicators for this text are GDP, the stock market, the housing market, and the unemployment rate. These particular indicators were chosen both because they are the most commonly used and because they represent particular flaws, though they are certainly not the only flawed indicators. The main point is to help the reader understand why the current methods or perceived methods for measuring economic strength are misguided and why the three methods proposed in the third section of the text are better. This understanding will only be clear when coupled with the lessons learned in the first section. This is another reason for including the opening section on Economics Island. It establishes the building blocks to understanding the ways in which the economic pie can be grown, which is another important concept of the book.

The final, and most important, purpose of the book is to establish three new economic indicators. It is almost inaccurate to call these measurements "indicators." Instead it is better to think of them as ways in which the economy can be strengthened. A good analogy is to think about these as ways to grow the economic pie. The premise that this section is built on is the idea of the perfect or ideal society that should be the goal of any economic system. This ideal society will be explained in more detail later in the book, but the basic idea is to aspire to a situation in which goods and services are unlimited with using the least amount of work possible. This allows for the maximization of choice, not only of which goods and services to utilize, but also the choice of how individuals use their time. This leads to the utilization of **productivity**, **efficiency,** and **trade surplus** as the three ways to get closest to this ideal society. The last section will show why these three measurements should be used to determine the relative strength of the economy.

II. Economics Island

In order to better explain the points in this book, I will use the reoccurring example of Economics Island. This fictional island will be the setting for the various characters used as a model to explain both simple and more complex economic theories. As in all economic discussion, there will be assumptions made to simplify the explanations. *Assumptions are a common tool of economic theoretical analysis that allow for simplified models to help explain naturally occurring economic principles. They allow the models and discussion to focus on one, or a few, economic principles without having to analyze everything all at once.* The situations will become more complex as the book moves forward. As in the real world, the size of Economics Island is fixed and the resources are scarce. A common definition of economics is the study of the allocation of scarce resources to their most efficient use. This means that the amount of natural resources and goods is less than infinity and therefore there is an optimum way to distribute them. Similarly the scarcity of resources on the island allows for a study based on efficient allocation.

The Barter System, Comparative Advantage, and Currency

Economics Island has one inhabitant: Alan. In order to survive Alan needs three basic things: food, shelter, and clothes. He collects his food in a berry patch on the island. He does this by simply picking the berries off the bushes. It takes Alan three hours to pick the berries he needs for the day. Next, Alan builds a shelter for himself. Every day Alan must work on the shelter for three hours to keep it up. Last, Alan makes clothing for himself, which also takes three hours. As he does for shelter, Alan must work on his clothing every day for three hours. In all, it takes nine hours for Alan to accomplish these three tasks each day. This is all the time he has because on Economics Island the sun is only out for nine hours and no work can be done in the dark.

Alan is then joined on Economics Island by Bob and Carla. The two new inhabitants like Alan must accomplish the three tasks to survive. Bob and Carla also take nine hours each to accomplish their tasks. The addition of the two new inhabitants does nothing to affect the economic well-being of the individuals on the island. The total amount of berries picked, shelters built and maintained, and clothes made, rises (by a factor of three) but Alan still takes nine hours to accomplish his tasks, still eats the same berries, lives in the same shelter, and wears the same clothes. The total amount of new houses, berries, and clothes on the island would be measured in the current world as Gross Domestic Product (GDP). *Gross Domestic Product, hereafter GDP, is a common measurement used to gauge economic strength. Almost every country keeps track of GDP and the totals are widely reported and studied. GDP is defined as the total market value of all final goods and services produced within a given geographical area, usually a country, in a given period of time, usually a year. The reason that it is measured in final goods is to avoid the problem of double counting. For instance, the value of the fishing rod is measured but not the value of the wood used to build the fishing rod. The formula often used to measure GDP is:*

C (Consumption) + I (Investment) + G (Government Spending) + X-I (Exports-Imports)

At this point on the island there is not any investment, government spending, or export/imports, only consumption. Therefore, GDP is simply the measure of consumption which on the island is the total amount of berries, shelters, and clothes consumed by the three island inhabitants. Here GDP would be higher while the economic well-being of the individuals would remain the same. This is because the consumption figure in the equation would triple now that there are three times as many as goods created (three times the berries, clothing, and shelter). At the same time each individual will still only have those three goods and Alan will have the same amount as when he was the only individual on the island. This apparent inconsistency is why GDP is an incomplete measure, but more will be said about this later in the book.

As time progresses on the island, Alan, Bob, and Carla become better at certain activities. Alan finds a new way to collect the berries so that it only takes two hours. He spends his extra one hour on leisure time, here defined as time not devoted to work. Again, more about leisure time will be discussed later in the book. Similarly, Bob shaves an hour off his shelter building time and Carla an hour off clothes making. With the improvements to their activities the three inhabitants have one extra hour each in which they do not have to be working. With these improvements and innovations, each inhabitant has created an expertise in one particular island activity.

The most efficient way for the island to operate, in light of the new comparative advantages of the inhabitants, would be to implement a barter system. If Alan were to spend all his time picking berries, Bob building shelters, and Carla making clothes, the inhabitants could shave more time off their total work output. Alan's saved hour would be multiplied by three, one hour for each person's berries. The same would be true for both Carla and Bob. Allen would pick the berries necessary for himself in two hours, the berries for Bob in two hours, and the berries for Carla in two hours for a total of six hours. Bob's and Carla's activities would similarly take six hours. At the completion of these six hours, Alan would trade Bob's allotted berries for the allotted shelter and Carla's allotted berries for his allotted clothes. Thus each inhabitant would have all their allotted goods in three hours less time.

The inhabitants' improvements in their particular task by itself only saved the group one hour of their individual work time, but when a trading system was implemented to their improvements, that one hour was multiplied threefold.

The above example shows the benefits of trade and comparative advantage. Individuals and societies have different expertise in different areas. It makes sense for these individuals and groups to perform the tasks they are best at and trade their goods or services to others who similarly have performed tasks that they are best at. A system that employs this kind of trading is more efficient than those in which each individual, or society, tries to accomplish every task on its own. The higher efficiency allows the work to be accomplished in a shorter period of time. *The amount of time it takes to complete a set amount of work is the measure of productivity.* Accomplishing the same amount of work in a shorter period of time equates to higher productivity. Higher productivity allows more goods and services to be produced and thus grows the pie, which is the ultimate goal of any economy.

Currency

The problem with the above example is the assumption that transaction costs are small. It is true that the overall work time is cut from eight hours to six hours when the improvements are coupled with a trading system. However, the trading system will take time that is not included in the work estimate. Also, not all goods are valued the same by unit. It is very difficult to trade goods and keep equilibrium. The situation is remedied by creating a currency which itself is worthless but can be used to value goods and services. The purpose of currency is that every good and service can be valued based on denominations of the particular currency. It is also easily moved and transferred.

As life on the island proceeds Alan begins to notice that it is very difficult to continually bring his berries over to Bob and Carla in order to conduct trading. He has also found it difficult to conduct trading with Bob because the shelter work is not extremely quantifiable. That is to say, the shelter improvements are continual while a day's worth of berries is finite. Alan decides that the way in which to remedy this situation is to create a currency. Being on an island covered with trees, Alan decides that the island currency will be made up of leaves. Each leaf is to be equal to one denomination of the currency hereafter entitled one leaf. Alan, Bob, and

Carla are now able to bring leaves to their transactions, instead of the cumbersome berries, clothes, and shelters, which makes them far more efficient. Alan begins to sell one bushel of his berries for one leaf, while Carla is able to sell a piece of clothing for five leaves and Bob is able to sell improvements to the shelters for ten leaves each.

The island inhabitants are now able to carry leaves around with them instead of their particular goods and services (which in most cases is very difficult and in Bob's case is impossible). They are also able to purchase the others' goods at any point without having to worry about offering a reciprocal trade at the same time. This allows Bob to be paid for his shelter improvements on a Monday and then use those leaves to purchase Alan's berries on Tuesday, Wednesday, and Thursday without creating disequilibrium of trade.

The above example shows the benefits and efficiency of adding currency to a barter system. The increase in efficiency occurs because of the decrease in time it takes the inhabitants to complete their respective trades. However, the above example is incomplete in that as presented it creates many problems along with its benefits.

The first issue with the leaves as currency is their abundance and lack of consistency. In essence it is the realization of the old saying about "money growing on trees." If the inhabitants are able to freely collect unlimited amounts of leaves used for exchange, then the leaves, in essence, become worthless. Why would Bob fix Carla's shelter for ten leaves when he can go out and collect ten leaves in his backyard? He could just as easily collect the leaves and use them to purchase Alan's berries without having to do the corresponding work needed to earn the leaves. Using the same logic, there is no reason for Alan to give Carla a bushel of berries for one leaf when he can collect one leaf from his backyard. A lack of a fixed centralized currency would break down all trade and return the inhabitants to the original system of individual work output.

The other problem, more easily remedied, is the issue of consistency of currency, mainly the threat of fraud in the exchange of leaves. The problem is in effect the extension of the problem of unlimited currency. If the inhabitants are able to forge the leaves that they are exchanging, there will be a similar breakdown in exchange. This forgery or creation of currency presents

the same problem as above by diluting the value of the actual currency in circulation.

In the United States the above problems are remedied by the presence of the Federal Reserve, also known as the Fed. The Fed is a central organization that prints and releases currency, which is the dollar in the United States. The amount of currency is not fixed in the sense of being static and unchanging, but fixed in the sense that it can only be placed into the economy by this one central organization. The Fed is able to place more dollars into circulation or remove dollars from circulation and this has various effects on the economy. The increase or decrease of the currency when done by a central organization, and not the individuals involved in the exchanges, keeps the barter system from breaking down.

On the island, the currency issue is remedied by employing a similar centralized organization, which changes the actual leaves into the currency version of the leaves. The organization is named by the inhabitants the Central Leaf Distributor, or "CLD." (The name of the organization is not important, nor should it be used to make any assumptions. Instead, it is simply used for ease

and convenience in describing the organization.) Leaves are collected and placed in the CLD where they are cut in a precise manner, to guard against fraud as is done with the dollar and all other paper currency, and then distributed to the inhabitants. With only three individuals on the island the best solution is for the CLD to distribute a set amount of leaves and no more. (The initial distribution does not follow a corresponding real-world example, in that the distribution of currency is normally done through the buying and selling of bonds. But to simplify the example, the inhabitants will simply be given the first allotment of currency.)

If more leaves are distributed past the original distribution, then the leaves will become less valuable and thus their purchasing power will decrease. This inevitably leads to the phenomenon of inflation; however, these subjects will be addressed later on. For now it is important to note only that a barter system supplemented by a currency system of leaves has been established on the island and that this system creates more efficiency than the previous system on the island. The currency needs to be limited and consistent in order to keep from creating a disincentive to trade. This is accomplished by creating a centralized organization to control the currency, on the island in the form of the CLD and in this country the Federal Reserve Bank.

Monopoly and Competition

At this point it becomes necessary to make an addition on the island of two new individuals: Dave and Erin. The island is still running on the barter and currency system as discussed in the previous chapter. Dave finds that he is best at making clothes, while Erin finds that she is best at improving shelters. Since Carla and Bob, respectively, already provide these services, competition is created.

Alan does not face any competition and thus has a monopoly on berry production. *Monopoly by definition is the absence of competition within a given market sector*. Alan's monopoly will be discussed in the next section.

Alan, like most consumers, feels comfortable with the familiar and so he continues to frequent Bob and Carla for the services he needs. Seeing this, Dave and Erin decide that in order to get Alan's business, and the leaves that come with it, they will need to lower their prices. Dave begins selling a piece of clothing for four leaves and Erin begins selling shelter improvements for nine leaves. This makes their goods one leaf cheaper than those of their respective competitors, Carla and Bob. Alan, although more comfortable with Bob and Carla, cannot resist the lower prices and begins to purchase his clothes from Dave and shelter improvements from Erin. Bob and Carla, seeing that they have lost business, have no other option than to lower their prices equal to those of their competitors, Erin and Dave. In situations like this, where supply outweighs demand, a price decreasing cycle is created. Since there is only one consumer, Alan, the incentive will always be for the inhabitants to lower their price below their competitors'. This downward pressure on prices will continue as long as the price of the good or service exceeds the cost of production of the good or service.

The above example leaves out two important factors of competition and pricing. The first is quality of service. It is not absolute that consumers will purchase their goods and services from the vendor with the lowest prices. Sometimes the consumer seeks the vendor whose quality of good or service is highest. Often the decision is based on some balancing of the two. However, the above example makes the assumption that the quality of services is the same between the two competitors. On the island both Carla's and Dave's clothes and Bob's and Erin's shelters are indistinguishable in terms of quality. Also, it is important to factor input costs into the calculation of prices. Although competition leads to decreases in price, as evidenced above, they can only be decreased to the point of their input costs. In other words, a vendor will not sell a good or service for a price less than it costs him to make or provide that good or service. The island inhabitants do not have input costs in the form of resources purchased because they collect all of the resources used for their services themselves. So, input costs for the inhabitants come in the form of opportunity costs which will be discussed after the below example.

Input Costs

Although the island inhabitants do not need to purchase their resources, an example where they do will be helpful in understanding input costs. Imagine Dave needs to purchase cloth for each of the pieces of clothing he makes. It takes one yard of cloth to make each piece of clothing. One yard of cloth costs two leaves. Dave's input costs are two leaves, meaning that in order to at least break even on his transaction he would need to sell the piece of clothing for two leaves.

To take the example one step further, imagine that Dave hires an employee to make the clothes for him. Dave has been very successful in trading his clothes and thinks he can pay his employee to make the clothes, giving him more leisure time, and still sell the clothes for more than his input costs. It is important to see that the input costs for Dave are now both the price of the cloth and the employee's wage. Dave has to price his clothing at an amount equal to, or higher than, the input costs of the wage and cloth in order to at least break even.

Opportunity Costs

Opportunity costs are those opportunities that you forgo in order to provide your service. In the inhabitants' case it is the forgoing of the other activities they could do which could net them more leaves. The reason Bob's service is clothes making is because he has a comparative advantage in making clothes versus collecting berries or improving shelters. However, if he lowers his prices to the point where the two hours it takes him to make clothes nets him less than two thirds the leaves he would receive for either berry collecting or shelter improvement, then his opportunity costs will be higher than his price. The opportunity cost here is in both leaves and time; however, it will be easiest to see using simply the time element. Bob is able to spend six hours making clothes in order to get his clothes, his berries, and his shelter improvements. He spends two hours on his clothes, two hours on the clothes he trades for his daily amount of berries, and two hours on the clothes he trades for his shelter improvements. The trade value of one piece of clothing is a daily amount of berries and a daily amount of shelter improvements.

Imagine that Bob lowers the trade value of a piece of clothing to one third of the daily value of berries and one third the daily value of shelter improvements. Bob still takes six hours to make the clothes but now only gets his clothes, one third of his berries, and one third of his shelter improvements. However, he still needs to get the other two thirds of both his berries and shelter. It still takes him three hours to get the daily amount of berries and shelter. So, to get the other two thirds of the berries and shelter will take Bob four extra hours; two for the remainder of the berries and two for the remainder of the shelter. Bob now must take ten hours to complete the work for the day. However, with no trading Bob could accomplish all his tasks in nine hours, so the opportunity costs for specializing in clothes at the new lower price are higher than the benefits of specializing. Under these new conditions, it makes more sense for Bob not to specialize in clothes. The above example shows how prices are based on both input costs and opportunity costs.

The lowering of prices by Dave and Erin and the subsequent loss of Alan's business forces Carla and Bob to similarly lower prices to an amount below those of Dave and Erin. This downward cycle continues as all four businesses approach their input cost totals. Fortunately for Carla she runs her business more efficiently than Dave and thus her input costs are lower. She is able to lower her prices to a level below Dave's input costs and is able to keep Alan as a customer. Bob and Erin both have the same input costs in building and maintaining their shelters and offer Alan the same price. However, Erin is more skilled at her job and has a better quality of service. With the prices the same, Alan chooses Erin based on her superior service and she is able to retain Alan as a customer.

The loss of Alan as a customer hurts Dave's business. He is still able to sell clothing to other inhabitants on the island but he is no longer making as many leaves as before. He realizes that if he took three hours to collect his own berries, instead of using that time to make clothes and using the leaves earned to purchase the berries, he would end up retaining more leaves. In this way, the opportunity costs of those extra hours worked making clothes are higher than the benefit he gets from the clothes made. He decides that he will collect his own berries and spend three less hours making clothing. The above examples show how competition, input costs, and opportunity costs determine pricing and the allocation of businesses within the market.

Monopoly

Alan, as a result of being the only island inhabitant distributing berries, has a monopoly on berry distribution in the market of the island. *Monopoly by definition is the absence of competition within a given market sector*. Here the market would be the island and the market sector would be berry distribution. There is a distinction to be made here between a monopoly and a natural monopoly.

A natural monopoly is one in which there is some existing set of circumstances that guarantees a certain vendor a monopoly. An example would be a farmer who owns the only land in which a certain product can grow. No amount of effort or ingenuity by other farmers could create competition for this product and thus the farmer is said to have a natural monopoly. Alan, on the other hand, only has a monopoly because he is the best berry picker and no one has attempted to compete with him. However, if one of the other island inhabitants decided to pick and distribute berries then Alan would no longer have a monopoly but instead would need to compete. The only way in which his monopoly could become a natural monopoly is if he were to be granted ownership rights through purchase, force, or regulation of all the berry patches on the island. If this were the case, it would bar any conceivable competition and create a natural monopoly. Natural monopolies work the same as other monopolies except for the lack of fear from possible competition. Since very few natural monopolies exist in the world, extensive analysis or examples from the island are not needed, though it is still important to understand the distinction.

Alan, not having any competitors, is able to charge for his berries whatever price he desires. His only determination is his consumers' willingness to pay. This price will be higher than the price that would exist if he was in competition. The natural spiral of decreasing prices in a competitive market was covered in the last section. As stated previously, this competition would bring the price down to the level of the input costs. In a monopoly this downward pressure does not exist and the prices will naturally be higher.

The difficulty in pricing is that individuals' willingness to pay for your good varies greatly. In the presence of competition the price is placed at a slightly greater amount than your input costs which allows those with a higher willingness to pay to take advantage of the lower price. Assume each vendor needs to make sales to two of the four other inhabitants on the island in order to be successful. Carla wants to price her clothing at the highest price that two inhabitants are willing to pay.

Assume that the willingness to pay for Dave, Bob, Alan, and Erin is three, four, six, and seven leaves, respectively. The willingness to pay is the maximum amount of leaves that each individual would pay for the clothing. Carla would like to price her clothing at six leaves and make sales to Alan and Erin.

Dave who is in competition with Carla would simply drop his price to five leaves to attract Bob; however, since prices are not discriminatory Alan and Erin will similarly buy from Dave, leaving Carla with no sales. *Prices are being described as non-discriminatory because they are advertised generally and not on an individual basis.* On the island it may be possible to barter your price effectively with each different inhabitant, but, in a market with a vast amount of customers, prices are fixed and advertised. So, the price you use for the person with the lowest willingness to pay is also the price used for the person with the highest willingness to pay.

As shown above, this will effectively drop both vendors' price to the level of their input costs. Monopolists do not face this same type of competition and downward pressure on prices. Assume Alan similarly needs to make two sales to be successful. Assume that the willingness to pay for a bushel of berries for Bob, Carla, Dave, and Erin is still three, four, six, and seven respectively. Alan will charge six leaves for his bushels of berries and will make the sale to Dave and Erin. The price will not come down in the absence of competition.

The above issue leads to the economic term "dead weight loss." This "loss" is the transactions that are not made because of the lack of competition and downward force on price. The amount of goods supplied by a given vendor will be the amount that can be provided at a price slightly above his input costs. Assume Alan has input costs of three and the willingness to pay for berries for Bob, Carla, Dave, and Erin is still three, four, six, and seven respectively. With competition Alan would sell his berries at some small amount above three, which we will call 3.5 for purposes of this example. Alan would sell berries for 3.5 to Carla, Dave, and Erin for a total of 10.5 leaves. Bob will not buy because the price is above his willingness to pay. However, in a monopoly Alan does not have the same pressure on his price point. He now chooses to sell his berries for six leaves. He will make sales to Dave and Erin for a total of twelve leaves. Even with Bob and Carla being priced out, Alan makes more money selling at the higher price. The dead weight loss is the efficient market transactions not made because of the monopoly, here the sale to Carla.

The other problem that arises out of a lack of competition is the lack of incentive for quality control. If Carla begins to slack off on her clothes making then her business will leave and go to Dave. Individuals on the island, if the prices are the same, will choose the highest quality clothing. This creates an incentive for Carla and Dave to keep the quality of their work high. However, if Alan does a bad job at collecting berries there is no one else for his customers to choose. There is not any substitute good that the island inhabitants can purchase to replace Alan's berries. Alan lacks the incentive to keep quality high because he has no fear of losing business. This lack of incentive for quality control is another negative of monopoly.

Supply and Demand

The theory of supply and demand is perhaps the greatest and most pronounced in all of economics. The supply and demand for a good or service directly correlates to its price. *Supply is the measure of the amount of a good or service that exists, while demand is the measure of the consumers' willingness to pay for the good or service. Equilibrium, representing the quantity produced and the price of the good or service, is the point at which supply meets demand.* Supply has a directly proportional relationship to price. The higher the price of the good or service the more the vendor will produce. Demand has an inverse relationship to price. The higher the price the less people buy the good or service.

Supply and demand can best be explained through graphs. The first graph below shows the basic supply and demand model with the equilibrium point of quantity and price identified.

Graph 1

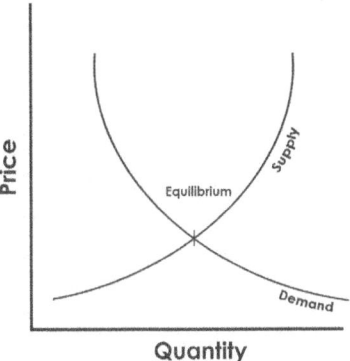

The next graph shows the progression of the equilibrium point when the supply curve is shifted to the right. The shift represents an increase in the supply and similar shift in equilibrium. Notice that with the increase in supply the equilibrium price decreases while the quantity increases.

Graph 2

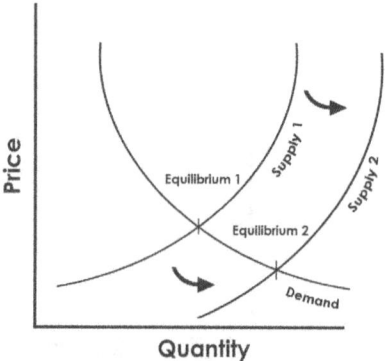

The last graph shows the progression of the equilibrium point when the demand curve is shifted right. The shift represents an increase in the demand and a similar shift in equilibrium. Notice as demand increases, both price and quantity similarly increase.

Graph 3

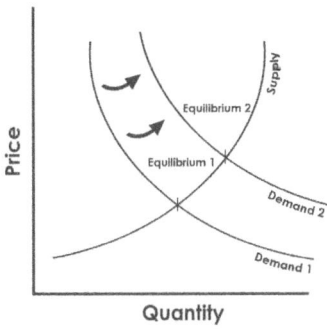

Price

Equilibrium 2

Equilibrium 1

Supply

Demand 2

Demand 1

Quantity

In analyzing the above graphs it is first important to explain why the curves look the way they do. The supply curve is directly proportional to price because as the price of a good increases the more people are willing to produce it. On the island, Alan is the only inhabitant to produce berries. This is because at the price of one leaf a bushel, only Alan can pick the berries in two hours and be successful. However, if the price of a bushel of berries was increased to two leaves it may become more profitable for one of the other inhabitants to pick berries. And if the price increased to three leaves it may become more profitable for two inhabitants to pick berries, and so on. As the price increases, the opportunity cost to switch to that occupation diminishes for the other inhabitants.

The demand curve is inversely proportional to price because as the price of a good increases, the less people are willing to buy it. At one leaf a bushel it is worth it for every inhabitant to buy their berries from Alan but if he increased his price to three leaves a bushel it may be better for the inhabitants to collect their own berries, which would decrease the amount of inhabitants willing to buy their berries from Alan.

The shifting of the curves represents a shock in either supply or demand. A shock in supply would come about if, on our island, Carla decided to switch from clothes making to berry picking. The supply of berries would increase, shifting the curve to the right. With the new influx of berries, there would be less competition among the consumers for the berries which would decrease the price. If there are only enough berries for two inhabitants of the island then they will bid against each other which will raise the price of berries. However, if there is enough for all five inhabitants then they have no need to bid which will keep the price low.

A shock in demand would occur if everyone desired twice as many berries while at the same time Alan produced the same amount of berries. This would create the reverse problem as in the above example, in that now there would be an increased bidding process for the berries. There would be only enough berries for half the inhabitants, so those who had a higher willingness to pay would bid higher which would increase the price.

Leisure Time and Innovation

The island inhabitants, up until this point, have only been producing three items: berries, clothes and shelters. This is because these three activities are necessities to survive and took the entire nine-hour work time to complete. Now, however, with the improvements in the economy, the barter system with the addition of currency, as well as competition created by the additional inhabitants, the three activities take less time. This extra time allows the inhabitants the choice to either enjoy more leisure time, with sleep and non-work activities, or produce more goods and services (or more likely some combination of the two). Either of these two options will provide innovations on the island. If the inhabitants choose to simply increase their leisure time they will need to fill this time with some form of non-work activity. The assumption is that the leisure time will not consist purely of sleep. For instance, the inhabitants may all decide that with their extra hour of leisure time they would like to fish, a reasonable activity for those located on an island. Three things would develop from this decision to fish; creation of a new product of fish, innovation in the technique of fishing, and the goods that come with the innovations in technique.

The assumption is that the decision to fish would result in the catching of fish. Fish, as the only other food item on the island besides berries, would become a tradable commodity, like the berries, clothes, and shelters. As with the other goods, invariably someone will be more talented in fish catching than the rest and will take fishing on as a profession. Inhabitants will change from less profitable tasks and move to fishing as long as it can sustain that many competitors in the market. As inhabitants move into the profession, competition will be created, which will lower prices and also spur improvement and innovation.

To illustrate this point, two new inhabitants, Frank and Gina, will be introduced to the island. Frank decided to compete with Alan in the berry business while Gina joined Carla and Dave in the clothes making business. Frank, however, was not as productive in gathering the berries as Alan. It took Frank more hours to collect his berries which made his input costs higher and correspondingly the price for his berries was higher. Gina also had a difficult time in making clothes, and so both decided to become fishermen. Gina became very successful at fishing and was able to catch six fish every day. Frank was not as successful and was only able to catch three fish a day. Because Gina is catching so many fish, the supply is increased and thus the price of the fish decreases. Gina is able to sell her fish cheaper and still afford the berries, clothes, and shelter she wants. However, at this price Frank is not able to afford the goods he needs. His options are to either move to another profession, as he did from berries to fish, or to improve his catching technique to be able to catch as many fish as Gina. In this pursuit, Frank develops the fishing rod, which will not only help him catch more fish and compete with Gina, but also sell the fishing rod which is now a new good.

The above example is oversimplified for explanation purposes. It would not be automatic that Frank would think to develop the fishing rod or be able to execute its design. However, with a much larger pool of people, the chance for innovation of this type becomes exponentially higher. The example illustrates how increases in productivity (i.e., the shrinking of the workday through barter and currency) lead to innovation (in the form of fishing and the fishing rod) and innovation leads to increased productivity (a decrease in the time it takes to catch fish). The innovation leads to new goods and services which provides more profession opportunities. It is not an increase in quantity but an increase in quality. Any inhabitant can take a profession, as anyone now can work. However, not all of these will be profitable. The fifth person who decides to pick berries is working but will not be able to sell any and will not make any leaves. But if a new job is created in which that person is the only vendor then he will become profitable. Imagine the seven inhabitants presently on the island with the four present jobs, at least three of the inhabitants will have to compete. But if three new professions are created so that there are seven professions, then the seven inhabitants will all be able to work in profitable professions. This is only possible with the progress of innovation. Taking this example one step further you can see a highly inhabited island in which inhabitants are not all working their own profession but instead working for other inhabitants. Innovation in this context would provide more jobs for the inhabitants.

The Stock Market

The island has now grown to include many inhabitants with many professions. Some inhabitants have begun selling natural resources on the island to those who need them for their profession. For instance, Erin had been collecting her own wood to make shelter improvements but now is buying her wood from Harry, another inhabitant on the island. Assume the island is in this state when Frank comes up with the innovation of the fishing rod. He develops the first fishing rod and is very successful in catching fish. He now wishes to turn his new invention into a profitable island business. In order to do so he needs to purchase wood from Harry. He does not have enough leaves saved up to purchase the wood he needs so he has to borrow leaves from other inhabitants.

The inhabitants will not give Frank their leaves without something in return. Frank agrees to give any inhabitant who gives him leaves an ownership interest in his new business. Frank needs twenty leaves to purchase the wood for his business. He puts in ten of his own leaves and gets five leaves apiece from Alan and Bob. In exchange Alan and Bob each receive a twenty-five percent (25%) ownership interest in the business. This entitles them to twenty-five percent (25%) of the profits.

Frank starts his business and is very successful. He is selling enough rods and has enough business to hire an employee, Isaac. His costs for each rod are two leaves for wood and one leaf for Isaac's labor. He is able to sell the rod for seven leaves, giving him a profit of four leaves per rod. In his first year he sells ten rods for a total profit of forty leaves. From this, Frank takes twenty leaves, fifty percent (50%) of forty, and Alan and Bob each receive ten leaves, twenty-five percent (25%) each of forty.

Another inhabitant on the island, Gina, believes that Frank's business will be even more successful in the following years. So, she offers Alan eleven leaves for his ownership interest in Frank's business. Alan agrees and the transaction is made. The inhabitants realize that a new commodity has been created. This commodity is the ownership interest in a business that can be bought and sold on the market like the other goods and services on the island. The inhabitants decide that these interests should be represented by a tangible object and choose bark from a tree. They also decide that the transactions should all be recorded in one central location in order to keep track of ownership. This central location is called the bark market.

The pieces of bark are governed by the market rules of supply and demand just like any other good or service. The supply of the pieces of bark is fixed and thus the price is indicative purely of the demand. The supply can be altered by a business offering more pieces of bark which would decrease the price; however, for this example we will assume that businesses are not increasing supply. The higher the demand for the pieces of bark (the more people who wish to buy them) the higher the price for each piece of bark. The total price of the bark market is simply a sum of the price of each individual piece of bark. Thus, an analysis of the total price of the bark market is only a measurement of people's willingness to buy bark.

For example, Erin has become very successful in her shelter building business and is looking to invest some of her leaves. She thinks that Frank has a great idea and that the fishing rod is going to be a real success on the island. She decides to buy bark in Frank's fishing rod business on the bark market. Harry, who sells his wood to Erin and thinks she is a very smart businesswoman, decides to follow her lead and invest his own leaves in the fishing rod bark. Alan, who has semi-retired from his berry picking business, is an avid follower of the bark market. He notices that the bark price for Frank's fishing rod business is rising quickly. Alan believes the price will continue to rise and decides to buy his own shares of bark. As we have seen before, this increase in demand will increase the price of the bark and by extension the bark market as a whole. However, the underlying company, Frank's fishing rod business, is no stronger financially than it was before Erin became interested. The bark price has risen simply on the belief of Erin, and by extension Harry and Alan, that the business would be strong in the future. This shows the bark market as a measurement of people's willingness to buy bark (demand) and not the actual strength of the company.

Interest Rates and the Price of Money

It is now important to focus on the role of the Central Leaf Distributor on the island. As discussed earlier the CLD is the central organization in charge of distributing leaves. In this role the CLD is affecting the supply of leaves. Leaves, like berries, clothes, and all the other goods or services on the island, are governed by supply and demand. This supply and demand affects the price of the leaves. Put another way, the supply and demand of leaves determines the amount of leaves a person is willing to pay for a leaf. This is a bit confusing; it would seem that a person would always pay one leaf for one leaf. However, when discussing the price of a leaf, the measurement is the willingness of an individual to pay a price in the future for the leaf now. In the real world this is commonly referred to as an interest rate. A person will borrow money with an agreement to pay it plus some percentage back in some future amount of time. Let us look back at Economics Island for an illustration of this principle.

Dave has seen how well Frank is doing in the fishing rod business. He thinks he has a good idea that could make him many leaves, but he does not have enough leaves saved up to start the business. He thinks about offering ownership in his company in exchange for leaves, like Frank did on the bark market, but decides he doesn't want other island inhabitants having any control over his business. Instead he offers Frank a deal. In exchange for Frank giving him ten leaves now to start his business, he will pay Frank back eleven leaves in one year. In this scenario, Frank does not need to worry about how well the company does because his leaves are not dependent on the business' profits or losses but instead on a guarantee from Dave. Now clearly, if the business fails, Dave may not be able to pay Frank back; however, in principle, without bringing in legal constructs, the payment is not contingent upon success.

In this example Dave was paying Frank an interest rate of ten percent (10%). He agreed to pay back the original ten leaves plus an additional one leaf which represents ten percent (10%) of the total loan. This price of leaves is measured in interest rates. In this case, Dave's willingness to pay was ten percent (10%). Because Frank is dealing with one person in a one-on-one transaction, he can negotiate and set a price for his leaves. After one year Dave pays Frank back. However, in the open market with many borrowers and lenders, the interest rate is based on the total supply and demand among all lenders and borrowers, and not individually negotiated. The interest rates in a large market are not negotiated individually but set for the entire market.

Frank now thinks that along with his fishing rod business it may be profitable for him to lend money out on a full-time basis. He must set a price for his good, leaves, in the same way he would set the price of any other good or service. He takes into account his supply of leaves and people's willingness to pay measured in interest rates (i.e., the demand), and calculates an interest rate. This price (interest rate) is set and now the good (leaves) has a price.

Monetary Policy and the Supply and Demand of Money

Next, it is important to focus on the role of the Central Leaf Distributor on the island. As discussed earlier the CLD is the central organization in charge of distributing leaves. In this role it is affecting the supply and demand of leaves on the island. We will start with demand by using an illustration from the island.

Frank is doing well in his new business and he has even taken on a partner, Bob. They renamed their business the Bank in honor of their two names. The Bank has been successful lending out leaves to other island inhabitants. However, Frank believes the Bank could be doing better if it had more leaves to lend. He looks to the CLD for help. The CLD will lend leaves to Frank's Bank at a certain price. The Bank, like any business, seeks to keep its revenue higher than its costs so the price it charges for leaves is based on the price the CLD charges it for leaves. Essentially, the interest rate charged by the CLD is the input cost for the Bank. In this way the setting of the price of leaves by the CLD will determine the price of leaves for the consumer. This price will affect the demand for leaves on the island. The CLD's choice of interest rate it offers to individual banks has a direct effect on the demand for money.

The CLD affects supply simply by deciding to put more leaves into the economy or to take leaves out of the economy. It does this by physically making new leaves and giving them to the inhabitants or by taking existing leaves away from the inhabitants. The more leaves that enter the island, the less each leaf will be worth. The reason for this is based on the necessity of leaves. As explained in the earlier chapter on the introduction of currency, leaves simply represent the value of goods in order to simplify transactions. Leaves do not have intrinsic value or worth except for the underlying good they represent. Every leaf on the island is tied to the valuation of the goods on the island. The total amount of leaves is equal to the total value of goods on the island. The leaves added by the CLD are automatically added into this valuation process. These leaves cannot stand alone without any purpose. If the CLD doubles the amount of leaves in circulation on the island then the price of goods on the island will similarly double.

This is what in the real world is called inflation. As the supply of money is increased the price of goods naturally rises. In the real world there is a lag in the rising prices but in principle, as on the island, increases in supply of money correspond to increasing prices. In this way each dollar is worth less. A dollar bill can buy a pack of gum for one dollar ($1) but if the supply of money is doubled then the pack of gum will jump to two dollars ($2) and that dollar bill is worth half as much as it was before. This is why an increase in the supply of money decreases the value of money and spurs inflation in prices.

International Trade

It is now time to introduce another island into the example and move away from the purely domestic and into the international economy. The island has now progressed to a fully functioning economy with a large amount of inhabitants. No longer are berries and clothes the only goods, or shelter building the only service. Through innovation, increased productivity, and a larger population, many new goods and services have been introduced into the island economy. Included in this new group of goods are ships that allow the inhabitants to travel beyond the island shores. During one of these seaward journeys the inhabitants discovered another island, similar to their own. This island, which the inhabitants called the other island, had similarly evolved into a barter economy supported by a currency. However, unlike Economics Island, the other island used sticks as their currency.

The inhabitants on Economics Island discovered that the other island was covered in a new food, which they did not have on their island, called coconuts. The inhabitants enjoyed the taste of the coconuts and desired them on Economics Island. At first they offered the growers leaves for the coconuts, but since the currency on the other island was sticks, the growers had no use for the leaves. The inhabitants then offered the growers a good that was not available on the other island; berries. In this way the islands traded coconuts for berries.

This example should seem familiar because it is simply the logical extension of the comparative advantage analysis used in the earlier section. The only difference is that now the comparative advantage exists between different islands as opposed to different inhabitants on the same island. This comparative advantage does not exist solely in situations in which the islands have different natural resources (coconuts and berries), but also in situations in which the islands perform different tasks better than the other; for example, the service of making clothing. Economics Island may have developed an innovative way to make pants that is desired by inhabitants of the other island. It is not that the other island cannot make pants or that they do not have the same resources to make pants, only that the makers of pants on Economics Island are more skilled. Here Economic Island has created a comparative advantage in pants making based on skill. The original example of comparative advantage is also one of skill, but instead of resulting in better quality, it results in lower costs.

The next part of this section will discuss differences in currency but for this example, an explanation will not be given. Imagine that both islands have fish and that they are the same quality fish. However, the other island has developed a new technique and better rod for catching fish. The other island is able to catch many more fish and thus they have an overwhelming supply on their island compared to Economics Island. Using the earlier explanation of supply and demand, the price of the fish on the other island would be less than that on Economics Island. The fish would be the same quality but the fish from the other island would be desired by Economics Island because of the lower cost. The other island has a comparative advantage in fish compared to Economics Island.

The next issue is analyzing the problems and solutions created by the difference in currency between the two trading islands.

Currency and Exchange Rates

Exchange rates are the values assigned to a particular currency in relation to another. For instance, using the U.S. currency (dollars) and the English currency (pounds), we can see the relative valuation of the two currencies. The way exchange rates are given is in the form _____ number of currency A = _____ number of currency B. Using our earlier example, we will use an exchange rate of two dollars ($2) equal to one pound (£1). This means that someone looking to exchange their dollars for pounds would have to give two dollars for every pound they would receive. So exchanging ten dollars ($10) would get the individual five pounds (£5).

In this way the mechanics of exchange rates are relatively easy.

However, the theory underneath the exchange rates is a little more complex. Again, it is important to remember that the currency, in our case dollars or pounds, is worthless on its own. The value arises out of the goods and services that the currency can purchase. Another example from the island, or in this case the islands, will be informative.

For this example, an assumption will be made that the only good available on both the island and the other island is berries. On the island, each bucket of berries costs one leaf, while on the other island, each bucket of berries costs two sticks. Bob who lives on the island was planning on taking a trip to the other island. He wanted to exchange his leaves for sticks so he would be able to purchase berries on the other island. Conveniently, for Bob and for purposes of our example, Sarah, who lives on the other island was planning on taking a trip to the island. Bob and Sarah get together to trade, or exchange, their currency. Bob and Sarah are both going to be on vacation for five days and will need to buy five buckets of berries each. Bob can buy five buckets for five leaves, so he brings five leaves to trade with Sarah. However, it takes Sarah ten sticks to buy five buckets of berries. For Bob to get equal value for his five leaves he will need to get ten sticks from Sarah. In this way, the exchange rate for five leaves is ten sticks, or reduced to its one leaf amount, which is how exchange rates are written, one leaf is equal to two sticks.

The above examples show the evolution of exchange rates. However, exchange rates are not static, they are continually changing. For instance, the dollar's relative value to the pound fluctuates depending on market circumstances. These fluctuations are based on both the current purchasing ability of the currency and the expected purchasing ability of the currency. If Bob was traveling to the other island for a longer period of time, for instance a year, he would need to make his exchange based on not just how many stick it costs to buy a bucket of berries today, but what he thinks it will cost in the future. These predictions are also made by those trying to make a profit on the open market. A particular currency can be an investment if it is expected to increase in relative value over a period of time.

For example, Bob believes that the CLD is going to increase the supply of leaves on the island. He knows that this increase in supply will decrease the price of leaves. He thinks that this decrease in the price of leaves will increase the relative value of sticks, the currency on the other island. For this reason, Bob decides to exchange some of his leaves for sticks. He does not intend to travel to the other island or use these sticks for purchasing, but instead simply as an investment tool. If Bob is correct and the CLD increases the supply of leaves and the relative value of sticks increases, he will have made a strong investment. He can later exchange his new sticks for leaves, this time at a more favorable exchange rate netting him an increase in leaves.

In this way exchange rates are simply market predictions of predicted inflationary tendencies. A particular currency loses or gains value comparatively to other currency based on its expected inflationary or deflationary tendencies in the future. If investors expect that the dollar is going to experience inflation in the future then the dollar will become less valuable compared to other currencies. This inflation can occur either because of an increase in the supply of actual dollars in circulation or because of a loss of confidence in the currency. The loss of confidence factor goes back to the intrinsic value of currency based on the ability to exchange. Individuals do not want to get stuck holding dollars if the dollar won't be able to be traded for any good or service. Usually this lack of confidence is a matter of degrees and not absolute, but to further illustrate the point an extreme example will be used.

Going back to our example from the islands; Sarah has just exchanged her sticks for leaves so that she can purchase berries on her trip to the island. On her trip she doesn't spend all of her leaves and so brings some home with her. She doesn't worry about spending all of her leaves because she knows she can go to the exchange store on the other island and exchange her excess leaves for the sticks she will use to purchase berries on the other island. However, on her journey from the island to the other island the government of the island collapses and the currency of leaves is disbanded. Now, berry vendors no longer accept leaves in exchange for their berries. If the leaves can't be exchanged for berries, then they are worthless. Sarah will not be able to exchange her excess leaves for any sticks. The exchange rate will be zero (or infinity, however you choose to look at it). Again, this is an extreme example, however, it shows why confidence factors into exchange rates.

The important point to take away from this section is that individual currencies have value relative to other currencies. These values change and are based on the supply and demand of the individual currencies. The supply is affected by the central currency distribution center, the CLD on the island. The demand is affected by both the price of the currency, dictated by the interest rate, and belief in its future value. These relative values are constantly changing based on the shifting levels of supply and demand.

Conclusion

Economics Island began with one inhabitant, Alan, responsible for finding food, building his shelter, and making his own clothes. Bob and Carla joined the island and through bartering and competitive advantage the three inhabitants were able to decrease their labor time while maintaining the same level of berries, clothing, and shelter. Next, the inhabitants developed a currency of leaves to make the bartering system more efficient. The CLD was created to control the supply and interest rate of leaves. Over time more inhabitants joined the island and through innovation, increased productivity, and efficiency, more products, businesses, jobs, and leisure time were created on the island. Businesses were thriving and investment began. To make this investment more efficient the inhabitants developed the bark market. Finally, the inhabitants began trading with the other island and through a similar system of comparative advantage and trading increased the economic standing of the island and the other island. This progression marks the evolution of the modern economic system and brings the island to a similar situation as our present-day society.

III. The Problem with Economic Indicators

The previous section of this book was devoted to the explanation of basic economic concepts using examples from Economics Island. The island was employed as an example for two reasons; first for ease and clarity of explanation, and second to remove conventional constructions of present-day economic thinking. It is difficult to conceptualize the role and effect of the dollar without first understanding that it is simply a tool to assess the underlying value of the goods and services being exchanged. Using the dollar, or any form of currency, brings more efficiency to an exchange then a simple good for good trade. The evolution of the island example allows the reader to better understand the functions and systems of the current economic system.

The rest of the book seeks to extend the understanding gained from the previous section with the goal of creating a new definition of a success. The reason for this new definition is that the current understanding of the economy and the indicators used to measure its strength and weakness is flawed. There are many current flawed indicators but this text will focus only on four: Gross Domestic Product (GDP), the stock market, housing prices, and unemployment.

Before moving forward with the new definition for success in the economy, it is first important to determine our goal. First, a distinction must be made. A common symbol used to explain economic theory is the pie. There are two ways in which to look at the pie; first, ways in which to split up the pie, and second, ways in which to increase the size of the pie. The remaining sections focus solely on the second view; increasing the size of the pie. This is not to say that it is not important to look at the way the pie is divided. Society may need to analyze the way in which its goods, services, and wealth (accumulation of the first two and currency) are distributed among its citizenry. However, the theory of this book is that a focus on distribution is purely societal and that the only economic goal should be the increase or decrease in the "pie."

But what is meant by "growing the pie"? Conventional wisdom is that it is the accumulation of wealth. The more wealth a society is able to produce and or acquire, the bigger its economic pie will be. This definition, however, is incomplete because it is purely quantitative. It is also important to determine the way in which the wealth is being accumulated. To see this it is necessary to discuss why the accumulation of wealth is desired. *Wealth is a measurement of goods and services.* It is usually used to describe currency, which as earlier reading explained, is just the means to acquire goods and services.

Goods and services are desirable for two reasons: they make labor easier and provide individuals with choices. In the beginning Alan was only eating berries, but then the new good of fish was discovered (created, meaning it was introduced to the market) and now he had a choice for eating. Similarly, the creation of the fishing rod made the labor of fishing easier. An extension of the easing of labor is the gaining of leisure time. The introduction of the fishing rod allowed the fisherman to catch the same amount of fish in less time. Now the fisherman could choose to work longer hours and catch more fish or to enjoy leisure time because of the fishing rod. It should not be interpreted that leisure time is simple idleness; instead it is time in which individuals can do what they want without consequence. For instance, Alan, at the beginning of his time on the island, might have had a choice as to picking berries, but if he did not he would die, which is really no choice at all. Leisure time, thus, is time in which he could choose to pick berries if he wanted, but would not have to in order to make a living.

If this definition of leisure is used, then it stands to reason that the goal of individuals would be to maximize leisure time. If it is time in which individuals can choose to do what they want, then the choice they make will be doing what they desire. Since individuals should want to do what they desire for the longest period of time possible, they should seek to maximize their leisure time. It is to this end that societies desire the acquisition of wealth.

Let us imagine the ideal situation, one in which the island, or any society, would receive every good and service that it could possibly want without having to do anything. This is a society in which every individual enjoys only leisure time. They are free to spend their time in any way they desire. If they want to labor they are free to, however, they do not need to because every imaginable good and service is at their disposal and in an unlimited amount. I would argue that this is the most desirable society and thus the goal of any current society. The question follows: what is stopping a current society from reaching the goal of the ideal society? The answer is time and scarcity. It has already been explained that resources are scarce. Goods and service are similarly fixed, but can be increased. The more goods that a society acquires the closer it moves towards the ideal situation described above.

Time is also important in moving towards the ideal society. If goods and services are increased at the expense of leisure time, then they do not move the society any closer to its goal. What benefit are unlimited goods and services if it takes all the individuals' time in society to produce them? Along with increasing the total amount of goods and services should be an emphasis on decreasing the amount of time it takes to produce these goods and services.

The economic goal of any society should be moving closer to the ideal situation described above by increasing the amount of goods and services while decreasing the amount of time for production. With this in mind, the success of the economy should be measured by only three indicators: efficiency, productivity, and trade surplus. These and only these measurements should be used to determine the overall health of the economy. Increasing these three factors should be the goal of any society looking to improve their economy.

The next section of the book will outline many of the current indicators and measurements that are used to judge the economy and give an explanation as to why I believe they are incomplete. The following section will give a further discussion of efficiency, productivity, and trade surplus and ways in which societies can improve upon these measures and thus the economy generally. The last section will provide concluding remarks on society's approach to its economy and the lessons learned from the island.

Gross Domestic Product (GDP)

Gross Domestic Product, hereafter GDP, is a common measurement used to gauge economic strength. Almost every country keeps track of GDP and the totals are widely reported and studied. GDP is defined as the total market value of all final goods and services produced within a given geographical area (usually a country) in a given period of time (usually a year). The reason that it is measured in final goods is to avoid the problem of double counting. For instance, the value of the fishing rod is measured but not the value of the wood used to build the fishing rod. The formula often used to measure GDP is:

C (Consumption) +I (Investment) + G (Government Spending) + X-I (Exports-Imports)

Consumption is the total measure of private spending by individuals within the economy. On the island this would be the measure of the total amount of leaves spent on berries, clothes, and other goods and service bought by the inhabitants. *Investment is the measure of total spending by individuals or businesses on goods used for investment purposes.* An example would be if a fisherman on the island purchased a boat to improve his ability to catch fish. Similarly, if Alan were to buy an extra berry patch in order to increase his profits this would be included in the Investment portion of the equation. Although described in common language as "investments," stocks, or bark on the island, would not be included in the Investment part of the equation. This is because the stock is used to buy intermediate goods which in turn are used to effectuate profits. For example, Frank uses the leaves he receives in exchange for the bark in his company to purchase the wood to build the fishing rods, or the boat to improve his fishing ability. The buying of stock is also not included in investment on the part of the individual. The bark represents the ownership right that is exchangeable on the market and therefore is not a good or a service itself.

Government Spending is exactly as it sounds; the total amount spent on final goods and services, including salaries paid, by the government. An example from the island cannot be given because a governmental form was not introduced to the example. This is partly by design, as the economic structure devised on the island does not need the existence of a government in order to function. This is the theory behind the free market. *The free market simply refers to a marketplace of freely exchanged goods and services that is unencumbered by any outside forces including, but not limited to, a governmental structure.* This book does not seek to debate political theory and therefore will not explore these ideas any further. On the island, government spending is zero and therefore does not affect the rest of the equation.

Gross Exports is the measure of the total amount of goods and services produced within the country and then exported outside the country. These are goods and services that the country is producing which are ultimately consumed by foreign countries. For example, the berries that are exported from Economics Island to, and consumed by the inhabitants of, the other island would be included within the Gross Exports portion of the equation. *Gross Imports is the measure of the total amount of goods and services produced outside the country and imported into, and consumed within, the country.* Gross Imports are not included to avoid inflated counting. For example, the coconuts that are imported and consumed by the inhabitants on Economics Island are included within the consumption measure of the equation. However, they are not produced within the country and therefore should not be, and are not, included within the GDP measurement.

Two issues arise with the use of GDP as a measure of the strength of the economy; the lack of attention to the time and effort required in producing the goods and services, and the emphasis on the domestic production of the goods and services as opposed to the domestic availability of the goods and services. Both are problems because they ignore the ultimate goal of the economy; reaching, or moving as close as possible to, the ideal economic society.

GDP is simply a totaling of the production of goods and services within the country. A higher GDP is seen as a sign of a stronger economy because of the benefit of having more goods and services. As explained in the introduction, the more goods and services available for consumption, the more choices available for individuals. Remember the ideal society is one in which there are unlimited goods and services available for consumption. However, GDP ignores the time and effort required to produce these goods and services. What good is increased production if it results in a loss of leisure time? Freedom and choice of goods and services is useless if individuals must spend all of their available time producing. Clearly a society would be better off if it was able to keep its GDP measurement constant while using less production time. Balancing the desire for a higher GDP and the amount of time needed to be spent in labor to create this higher GDP is a worthy debate for societies to have, but the time element must be included in order to have an accurate reflection of economic strength.

The second problem is based on a similar rationale. It exists with the emphasis on domestic production as opposed to domestic availability. *Domestic production is the measure of goods and services produced within the given geographic area.* On the island this would be all of the berries picked, shelters built, clothes made, etc. *Domestic availability is the measure of the amount of goods and services that are actually available for consumption by individuals of the given geographic area.* If the point of goods and services is to give choice and freedom to individuals for the purposes of consumption, then shouldn't the emphasis be on the goods and services *available* for consumption? What does it matter how many goods and services are produced by a society if the individuals living within that society cannot consume them? The problem is inverting gross imports and gross exports in the GDP equation. Imports are excluded because they are produced in a different country. However, these imports are goods and services that can be consumed by the individuals of the country and thus should be included in any measure of how well the economy is doing. The exports, although produced within the country, cannot be consumed by the individuals of the country and therefore should not be included in the equation.

For example, on Economics Island GDP is calculated using the above formula Consumption + Investment + Government Spending + (Exports–Imports). Consumption on the island consists of all the berries, clothes, shelters, fish, and fishing rods purchased by Alan, Bob, Carla, Dave, Erin, Frank, Gina, and Harry. Investment consists of all the wood (used for fishing rods) and coconuts (used for berry picking) purchased by Frank's fishing rods business and Alan's berry picking business. There is no governmental entity on the island and thus government spending is zero. Exports are all of the berries that Economics Island sent to the other island, while imports are the coconuts sent from the other island to Economics Island. There are many ways to increase GDP on Economics Island; however, not all of them would strengthen the economy. For instance, if the relative value of coconuts increased compared to berries then Economics Island would need to export more berries and would be importing less coconuts. This would increase the (Exports – Imports) total and increase total GDP, but it would not strengthen the economy. Similarly, if Alan became less efficient in the way he used coconuts to pick berries, he would increase his investment in coconuts to produce the same total of berries. This would increase the investment total and overall GDP, but it would not correlate to a stronger economy.

This example from Economics Island and this section as a whole show the problems with using GDP as an indicator of economic strength. There are benefits to using GDP as an economic measurement, but only if its limitations are understood. Later in the book Productivity, Efficiency, and Trade Surplus will be discussed as alternatives to the current indicators, but first a look at the stock market, the housing market, and unemployment.

The Stock Market; as an indicator

The stock market is another indicator commonly used to gauge the strength of the economy. A detailed explanation of the stock market is not needed as one has already been provided in the first section of this text. Many complexities are contained within the meaning of stocks and the stock market. Over time, many tools and financial devices have been created and employed for the purposes of both efficiency and increased profits. These new financial devices are simply a product of market evolution and innovation, similar to that of any other good or service. So as the service of providing fish evolves into the development of a fishing rod, so too does the sale of a simple ownership right on a common market evolve into the selling of many ownership rights to credit in the form of bundled mortgages. These new financial devices and techniques are important to the everyday functions of the stock market; however, they are not important to the fundamental understanding of the market or why it is a flawed indicator for overall economic strength. Using this determination, the market will be discussed simply using the buying or selling of basic common stock.

A common stock, hereafter referred to only as a stock, is a representation of ownership in a particular business or company. The amount of stock an individual owns compared to the amount of stock issued determines the amount of ownership in the company. For instance, if Company A issues one hundred stocks, one hundred representations of ownership, and an individual owns one stock, then he has a one percent (1%) ownership interest in the business. The pieces have value in two ways; first in the monetary gain that can arise from company dividends and second the potential increase in the price of stock at sale compared to the price bought. Dividends are the payments made to stockholders by companies, usually at given intervals of time. Often, dividends are reflective of profit so as profits increase, dividends similarly increase. Stockholders as owners of the company expect to be rewarded for their initial investment with portions of the profit. In our example if the company makes a profit of $100 then the individual with the one percent (1%) stock interest will expect a payout of $1. This relationship is based on the original way in which the investment for ownership interest occurred. As examined in the earlier chapter on the island's bark market, businesses in need of initial capital offered an ownership right in their company in exchange for needed funds. This ownership right eventually evolved into a commodity which was bought and sold on a common market. In this way the dividend as a portion of profit became less important compared to the speculative nature of the market. A speculative market simply refers to the fact that stocks are bought and sold based not just on their current value but on their expected future value.

The second value, an expectation of appreciation, is no different than any other good that can be bought and sold in the market. The owner of the stock anticipates an appreciation in the price based on an increased demand. The increased demand, as discussed earlier, will increase the price, thus accruing a monetary gain for the stock owner. This increased demand can occur for many potential reasons. The company that the stock represents could improve its bottom line, thus offering a higher dividend or promise of a higher dividend. The company could increase its potential earning power through a new product, a merger or acquisition, the hiring of a new manager, etc. The company could simply become more famous or popular, through new and favorable coverage or word of mouth. Or, the demand for stocks in general could increase based on perceived economic strength which would increase the demand for individual stocks.

This was shown in the example from Economics Island where Erin bid up the price of the fishing rod bark (stock) based on her belief that it would be a strong company in the future. This led to Harry and Alan purchasing bark in the company which only further increased its price, all without the company making any changes to its production or profit.

Individuals choose to buy stocks on the common market with the intention of being profitable. They may believe in the company whose stock they are buying or simply that the stock will go up in price. This determination could be made based on either the individual stock's strength, or the strength of the market as a whole. The more individuals that choose to buy a stock the higher that stock's price will be.

The stock market as an indicator of the U.S. economy is usually measured by the points of either the New York Stock Exchange or the NASDAQ market. Both are markets on which U.S. stocks are traded, with the NASDAQ focusing on more technology stocks. For purposes of this discussion the differences in the markets do not matter and both will be lumped together and referred to generically as the stock market index. The stock market index is measured by choosing a certain number of stocks within the market and tracking their price. These stocks are reflective of the market as a whole, and as their prices fluctuate, it is assumed, the market as a whole similarly fluctuates. This index is then given a number, measured in points, which goes up and down as the stock prices within it go up and down. So, when the stock market is said to be down, it is because the prices of these representative stocks are down.

As discussed earlier, stock prices are entirely reflective of supply and demand. The less people willing to buy a stock, the less demand there will be for the stock. Similarly, the more people wanting to sell the stock, the more supply of the stock there is. If the supply is increased and the demand is decreased the price will decrease. This is an important point to emphasize. The price of the stock decreases simply because of the desire of the individuals within the market to sell more and/or buy less of the stock. The converse is also true; if more people choose to buy a stock and/or less choose to sell that stock, the price will increase. This happens continually in the market. People buy and sell stock in companies for many reasons. These reasons can often be based on the performance of the company. This is the way the stock market, and all markets, are supposed to work. Those companies that are successful should continue to operate and receive financing while those that are unsuccessful should cease to receive funds until they improve or are replaced in the market. However, individual investors don't have full knowledge and often make uninformed choices. Many times, these choices are based on the conventional wisdom of the moment. This is also true of every market, but more commonly in the stock market; where individuals have less understanding of the companies and financial instruments they are buying and selling.

It is the lack of knowledge and panic-based decisions that lead to the problem of using the stock market to measure economic strength. A sudden or prolonged drop in the index is usually used as a rationale for describing the weakness or weakening of the economy. However, it is really just a measurement of the subjective impression of the market, or the economy as a whole, of the individual investors. This is not to say that this subjective impression is always wrong. It can be, and often is, right. However, enough decisions are made using this subjective and faulty analysis to render the use of stock market fluctuations a poor indicator of economic strength or weakness.

Housing Market

The housing market, like the stock market, is no different than any other market in the economic structure. It does have certain characteristics that distinguish it from other markets, such as the infrequency with which homes are bought and sold, and the high ratio of spending on homes in relation to overall spending. However, this does not change the basic elements that make up all markets, specifically that the price of housing is entirely based on the supply and the demand for it within the market. That is to say, the more housing built, (the amount of total structures) if demand remains the same, the lower housing prices will be. The higher the demand, (the amount of housing desired by individuals) along with their ability to pay, holding supply steady, the higher housing prices will be.

The housing market has some unique characteristics that lead to it being viewed more as an indicator than other markets. First, it is an infrequently purchased good. Unlike food, clothing, or even luxury items such as electronics or vacations, an individual or family will probably only buy two or three homes over the course of their lifetime, and some will not buy any. Similarly, the cost of housing is higher than any other single purchase individuals make. It will often account for up to a third of an individual or family's spending for the year.

Second, housing is a completely domestic good. It is not imported from, or exported to, foreign countries. It is true that the supplies used to build housing are imported and exported but the final structure, the only item being measured, is completely domestic. There are some circumstances when entire structures are shipped between countries but this is such a rare occurrence that it will not be addressed and does not factor into the market determination. The lack of exportation is important because it removes the element of competition between markets. It is true that there is still competition between regional markets, as in the southwest compared to the northeast, but because the housing market is measured on the national level when judging the strength of the economy, the lack of international competition is important.

The final defining characteristic of the housing market is that individuals are not only consumers but also sellers. The original sale takes place in the normal scenario in which the business producer sells to the individual consumer; however, all subsequent sales of that housing unit are made between individuals. And unlike most goods, housing usually appreciates with time, or at least does not automatically depreciate with time as most other goods do. In this way, housing as a commodity is like a stock; it is not only worth its current use but also its potential future selling value. As in the case of stocks, buyers make determinations about the level of value others will have for the housing unit in the future. Similar to the stock market, individuals are more concerned with the overall status of the housing market because of its effect on the future sales value of the house they own.

The housing market is different from the stock market in that its overall strength is based not only on the price of the individual homes within it, both new and existing, but also on the amount of sales made within the market. For example, in a scenario in which a very limited amount of people chose to buy stock and no one chose to sell stock, prices would go up and the market would be said to be "up." However, in a similar circumstance in which a very limited amount of people chose to buy homes, and very few chose to sell, although housing prices would increase (due to increased demand and limited supply), the lack of transactions in the market may result in a determination that the market was "down." Stocks are bought and sold to make a profit and for investment purposes. Most people buy and sell homes as a life decision and the inability to make these transactions has a negative impact on their lives. Further, because home buyers usually need to first be home sellers, their inability to sell their homes may stop them from buying homes. This spiral continues and has a negative impact on demand which lowers prices. This is generally not true for the stock market. Thus, in looking at the housing market as a measurement for the strength of the economy, both overall price and amount of transactions must be taken into consideration.

Overall price in the market, as with stocks, is determined by the prices of the individual homes within the market. Again, for this analysis the term "housing market" will describe the national, and not regional, markets. The price of each individual home is determined by the demand for that particular home, the overall demand within the market, and the overall supply within the market. It is easy to see how the demand for that particular home would affect its price. The more desired the house is, the more people will bid for the ability to buy it, which will increase the price. However, overall demand also determines the price of the home. For example, assume that there are three houses on a block. If there are only two potential buyers for those three homes, then the ugliest house of the three may not even receive any offers. However, if there are ten potential buyers, after the first two homes are purchased, the ugly house will be the only house available. The eight remaining buyers will be forced to bid on this house, if they still wish to buy a home, which will increase the selling price of the house.

This example also works as an explanation of why overall *supply* affects the price. Assume that those same ten potential buyers still exist, but now there are ten available houses on the block. The ugly home may only get one offer from the tenth buyer; with no bidding process and only one potential buyer, the price will decrease.

The individual demand for a particular home can be based on many things, all of which are subject to that home and the potential buyers in that area. An analysis of individual demand is not needed because it is purely subjective and has no relation to the relative strength or weakness of the economy. However, an analysis of both overall demand and overall supply is needed. Because the analysis for price increases and decreases is the same, just reversed, and because housing price decreases are less common and are viewed as more correlated with a weakening of the economy, only housing price decreases and their causes will be analyzed.

Overall demand is the total willingness, of buyers in the market, to purchase homes in the market. Demand is measured both by the amount of people wishing to buy, and their willingness to pay. For example, an increase in demand can occur if the amount of people wishing to buy homes increases from four people willing to spend up to $100,000 each, to six people willing to spend up to $100,000 each. It can also increase if the amount of people wishing to buy homes remains constant but their willingness to spend is increased from $100,000 to $200,000. In this example of a decreasing housing market due to decreasing overall demand, the cause could be less people wishing to buy homes and/or a decrease in the amount people are willing to spend on housing, or both.

There are many reasons why a decrease in the amount of people wishing to buy a home could occur. These reasons do not differ from those that govern demand for other goods. Mainly, the good could become too expensive, a substitute good could gain appeal, or individuals could be content in their present situation. These same reasons apply to housing; the cost of buying a home could become too expensive; a substitute, in this case apartments and/or other rent-seeking properties, could emerge, or individuals could be content in the homes they currently live in and lack a desire to change.

It is important to evaluate what is meant by "too expensive." This is not merely a monetary measurement. Price is irrelevant in a vacuum; it is only significant in relation to wage and wealth. For instance, the price of a house may increase from $100,000 to $125,00, but, if during that same time the individual who is considering buying the house has a wage increase from $10/hour to $15/hour then the house will be "less expensive" at the later price. It is also instructive to use an example from the island to make the point more clearly by removing dollars from the example.

Imagine Alan is able to purchase a shelter from Bob in exchange for twenty berries and it takes him a full day to pick twenty berries. Now imagine Alan is able to speed up his picking process so that in a full day he can pick one hundred berries. Assume Bob increases the amount of berries it takes to purchase a shelter to fifty berries. That is a net increase of thirty berries; the price in berries is over double what it was before. However, it will only take half a day of work for Alan to purchase the shelter. The total amount of berries to purchase the home increased, but Alan's salary (berries collected) has now increased at a greater rate and thus the house is relatively less expensive for him to purchase. This example shows the relation of housing price and salary, or more precisely labor hours needed to purchase the house, for one individual on the island. It can easily be extended to all individuals on the island, in that if total salaries are rising at a faster rate than housing prices, housing costs become less expensive even when gaining in overall price. In this way, when looking at demand for housing it is important to look not only at price, but price in relation to wage, or even more accurately in relation to the amount of work needed to gain that wage.

A relative increase in price compared to wage is based on a shift in the relative valuation of housing compared to the good or service provided by that wage earner. Again, it is instructive to use an example from the island. Alan can purchase one shelter from Bob at the rate of twenty berries. Shelter and food are both important and this represents an even trade of the two items. However, assume that the island is then plagued with a storm season. Now housing becomes more imperative and is valued higher than berries. Clearly food is still important, but an island inhabitant now values a roof over his head in a storm more than some extra berries for added nourishment. In this example the price of housing increases relative to the wage of the berry producer, which is simply the price of berries. In this example of a storm season, the same change in valuation with all island products, with the exception of specialty storm-related ones, would decrease in relative value to housing. So, housing prices would increase relative to the whole market. This change in valuation could happen in the other direction. In that same example, the island inhabitants could discover coconuts, which would make berries less needed and less desirable. Berries would be valued less and their relative value compared to all products, including housing, would decrease.

A change in relative valuation can also occur due to a readjustment after a speculative bubble. Speculation is a common practice used for economic gain. *It simply means the acquisition of a resource or good, often land, not based on its current value but on its future value.* The goal in speculating is to buy at the current cheap price and then sell at the higher expected future price. Speculation is frequently used on the stock market, where a stock is bought based on an expectation of future profits that would allow the stock to be sold for greater than its current buying price. Two of the most popular examples of speculation, at least in the United States, are the gold and oil rushes. The gold rush started in 1848 when gold was discovered at Sutter's Mill in California. The news traveled, and men and women began flooding to California in search of a gold fortune. Between 1848 and 1855 more than 300,000 individuals traveled to California in search of gold. The rush for oil was similar, if not as iconic in American story-telling, instead occurring in the late 1800s and early 1900s but still mostly out west. Speculators bought up large tracks of land hoping that oil could be found underneath, to not only pay for the land but also make large profits for these speculators. Sometime it wasn't even the oil drillers who would speculate on the land, but individuals hoping to sell to oil drillers.

These two examples are interesting, not only for their historical significance, but because they help illustrate the way in which speculative bubbles drive up prices unnaturally and the resulting falls that inevitably take place. People moving to California, looking for gold or oil, are purchasing land not for its current value but its potential value due to the possibility of finding gold or oil. As more people move into these places the demand increases and the willingness to pay increases. Individuals, blinded by the notion of mass fortunes, compete for the limited amount of land and bid the prices up exponentially. It is not just the land where the gold or oil is thought to be, but all land in that geographic area, that increases in value. The surrounding land is needed for homes, both for the speculator and for his workers. For example, a piece of land may be worth $100 as a potential home site before the rush. That is the price at which individuals are willing to spend in order to buy the land and build a home. However, as a potential spot to dig for gold or drill for oil, it is now worth $400 to a speculator who thinks he can make a substantial profit.

It is important to remember that speculation does not necessarily run counter to the normal market price. A discovery of gold or oil on a nearby piece of land should increase the value of the surrounding land. Gold and oil can be sold in the market and thus increase the price of the land beyond its normal value. However, the land should be valued by the potential value of the oil or gold that could be collected together with the percentage of finding it. This is because gold and oil being discovered on nearby land may increase the chances of discovering gold and land on surrounding properties, but does not guarantee it. The problem occurs in speculation when the second part is left out of the valuation decision of individuals. In situations of vast speculation, individuals assess the value of the surrounding land based on unrealistically high percentages of discovery. Individuals by nature want to imagine that their life can be changed by a great stroke of luck. Studies have shown that when mass fortune is involved, people assign an unrealistically high percentage of luck to themselves. When this happens, the price of the speculative good, in this case land, rises to an unnaturally high level. After the speculation and exuberance die down, the market forces take over and the price returns to a natural level. This is an example of how speculative bubbles can lead to a readjusting period and a decrease in prices.

The second reason for a decrease in overall demand is the presence or emergence of a strong substitute good. A substitute good is one that can be used or enjoyed in place of another. For instance, to borrow a classic example, margarine is used as a substitute for butter. Most substitute goods can be used only in certain similar situations, and only to a certain degree of success, as the good they are being substituted for. Perfect substitutes are goods that can be used in exactly the same way as the good they are replacing. The soft drinks of

Pepsi and Coke are usually cited as an example. The idea being that if Coke were taken off the market, Pepsi consumption would increase by the exact amount that Coke decreased, leaving overall Coke-type beverage consumption constant.

In housing, the substitute goods are apartments or similar rent-seeking residences. *In this example housing is being used to describe all living structures in which individuals can gain an ownership right.* All individuals wish to have shelter. In choosing shelter, the decision is between housing, as defined above, or the substitute to housing, apartments and similar rent-seeking residences. A shift in valuation from housing to apartments can come either from a decrease in the relative price of apartments or from societal changes making apartments more attractive. A decrease in the relative price of apartments results in a higher demand for apartments and a corresponding decrease in demand for housing. When housing is demanded more, apartments experience a similar decrease in demand. This decrease in demand leads to a decrease in price, as less people are bidding for the use of apartments, and thus the cycle begins again. In this way, the markets for housing and apartments are interrelated and constantly shifting back and forth in relative valuation.

Societal shifts can also skew the valuation of apartments to housing. For instance, as individuals move to the cities the demand for apartments increases, resulting in a similar decrease in housing demand. Also, a shift towards a more transient society would cause a need for rent-seeking, as opposed to ownership, properties and increase the demand for apartments.

The final reason for a decrease in overall demand is the desire of individuals to stay in their current residence instead of moving. Individuals and families have many reasons for remaining in their current housing, one of which is the price of moving to alternate housing. Similar to the analysis above, if the relative cost of housing is too high the demand for it will be lower. Here, the analysis of the housing market is different than other markets because exchanges are made not simply for profit. Buyers may desire the same amount of housing but simply do not desire new housing. Clearly, new entrants to the market, those without current housing, would still demand housing, but this is only a percentage of housing sales and thus overall demand would decrease.

Overall demand for housing is only half of the equation in determining price. The other half is overall supply. An analysis of individual supply is superfluous because either the individual house is on the market, meaning the supply is greater than zero, or it is not on the market meaning supply is zero. Clearly in the latter situation there will be no price and so individual supply does not affect price. Overall supply, like overall demand, is the total amount of supply within the market. *In the housing market, based on the definition used in this text, the overall supply of housing is the total amount of housing structures placed on the market for sale, which is simply a transfer of ownership.* Supply for housing can occur in two forms: new construction or existing homes. Although both have an effect on supply and therefore price, there are differences between the two.

Existing homes placed on the market increase the supply of housing available for purchase. This increase in supply, holding demand constant, will decrease the price of housing. For instance, if five people wish to buy homes in a neighborhood with five homes for sale, the fifth individual will have equal negotiation power with the seller of the fifth house. The equal negotiating power exists because each needs the other equally to achieve their goals of buying and selling a home respectively. The only way the fifth individual can buy a home in this neighborhood is if he buys it from the owner of the fifth house for sale. Similarly, the only way the fifth house can be sold is if the fifth buyer purchases it. However, imagine that now there are ten houses for sale in the neighborhood. Now the fifth individual has six houses to choose from. The owner of the fifth house now has to compete with the five other homeowners in order to sell his home. This competition and advantage in negotiation power of the buyer results in the owner of the fifth house lowering the selling price. This example extended over the whole market shows how increases in total homes for sale lower prices universally.

An increase in new home construction has the same effect on supply and price as the above example. However in new home construction, there is an absolute increase in supply. Conversely an increase in existing homes is just an increase in transactions. This stems from the nature of the housing market in which the producers are both commercial (new home construction) and individual (existing home sales). When existing homes are placed on the market it is usually followed by the owner of that home seeking a new home herself. (Clearly this is not always the case, as many existing homes sold are not the primary residence of the seller.) In this scenario transactions within the market are increased, and the increase in supply is combined with an increase in demand. The increased demand is from the sellers who become buyers. This has a mitigating effect on the decrease in prices. In comparison, the increase in supply due to new home construction increases the total amount of available housing, not just the transactions. This is not automatically combined with an increase in demand and thus the decrease in price is more drastic. The important point to take away is that an increase in supply, either through more existing home sales or new home construction, results in a decrease in price.

It is necessary to understand these reasons for decreasing prices when analyzing the relation of the housing market to the strength of the economy as a whole. The conventional wisdom is that if the housing market is down, either through lower home prices and/or a fewer number of transactions, then it is a sign the economy as a whole is weakening. The analysis above shows that this is not necessarily true. The lower price could simply be a factor of decreased demand based on changing valuation. Typically, this occurs following a period of speculation in the market. In these situations, the decrease is not a sign of weakness but a natural correction in the market. In fact, it is a positive correction because the prices in the speculation period are not natural and not sustainable. Even if the decrease is not preceded by a speculative period it may simply be a reassigning of valuation. Individuals are constantly adjusting their determinations of valuation for goods in the market. This is true across entire markets. This adjusting of valuations is the reason why markets are dynamic and prices are constantly increasing and decreasing.

The emergence of a substitute good is also not a negative. In fact, an argument can be made that the more options and choice presented to individuals looking for housing, the better. The relative valuation between owned homes and apartments is constantly shifting. As the demand for one increases, the price will increase. This increase in price will cause the demand for the now less expensive substitute option to increase which in turn will increase its price, beginning the cycle all over again. This cycle repeats itself constantly and results in the constant shifting of relative valuation.

Similarly, an increase in supply is not a sign of a weakening economy. If anything, more housing options should be seen as a positive. If the goal of any economy is to reach the ideal society in which all possible goods and services are provided with the least amount of work possible, then an increase in available housing should be seen as a step in this direction. If increased supply is due to more new homes being built, then it is a sign of a strong building industry. If it is due to increased existing home sales it is a sign of individuals' confidence in the market. As explained in the section on the stock market, individuals' confidence is not automatically correlated to a corresponding strong or weak economy. It is important to remember these root causes of decreasing prices when analyzing their relation to the economy as a whole.

As mentioned earlier, the housing market is different because its supply is provided both by commercial interests (new home construction) and individuals (existing home sales). This is important because it explains why sinking housing prices are felt by individuals as well as commercial interests. However, like all other markets, consumers benefit when prices decrease. As much as the individual selling the home is negatively affected by the decrease in prices, the individual buying the home is positively affected.

This section of the text is dedicated to the analysis of current economic indicators as measures for economic strength. Specifically when dealing with housing it is important to understand the root causes of both supply and demand that determine the price of housing stock both individually and as a whole. While housing operates under the same market conditions as other goods and services it does have some unique defining characteristics; it is infrequently purchased, completely domestic, and has individuals operating as both buyers and sellers. Finally, the strength of the market is based not just on housing prices but also frequency of transactions. Typically decreasing prices and infrequent transactions is described as a down market and corresponds to a down economy. This is not always true and must be analyzed based on the conditions that lead to the decrease in price and transactions. More housing options at decreasing prices are steps towards the perfect society and thus should not be looked at as a weakening of the economy.

Unemployment Rate

Employment, loosely defined, is a position held by an individual in which she is compensated in exchange for work.   Unemployment is the term given to the status of not being employed.   Unemployment is typically measured by the unemployment rate.   This rate is calculated by dividing the total number of eligible workers by the amount of workers currently unemployed. The number is given in terms of percentage. Unemployment rates vary depending on the geographical area in which they are measured. The average rate in the United States is around six percent (6%).

Unemployment on its own is not necessarily a negative economic scenario. Employment is not an end by itself but instead a means to achieve an end, in this case obtaining goods and services. The problem occurs when unemployment is coupled with the scarcity of goods and services.   In the perfect society, outlined earlier in the book, a shortage of jobs would not be a problem because all goods and services would still be provided. An argument could be made that this lack of jobs would limit choice, which is an element of the perfect society; however, the ability to perform the functions of the jobs would still be available, just without the compensation, which would have no effect on choice. For example, imagine the island reached the level of the perfect society, where all goods and services were available at no cost and at an unlimited level. Bob could no longer sell his shelters because there would be unlimited shelters available for free and no one would pay for a good they could get for free. However, Bob is not limited in choice because he could still build shelters (perform the functions of his job), he would just not be paid for building them. Again, he would not need to make money from his shelter building because all goods and services would be free and he would have no need for money. This example is just to illustrate that the lack of need for shelters does not prevent Bob from building them, if that is what he wants to do.

Clearly, the current society has not attained this perfect level. Goods and services are scarce, as a result of underproduction. Society never produces enough until this perfect level of production, being the point at which goods and services are unlimited. Up until that point, society is under-producing. One cause of this underproduction is an inefficient use of resources. High unemployment signals an inefficient use of the resource of human capital. Each unemployed body could be utilized in producing a new good or service and any amount under full employment for this purpose signals inefficiency.

Institutional unemployment is the name given to the percentage of the population that is deemed unemployable, often the very young or those that are physically or mentally lacking in some way that makes them unable to be productive in any type of work. This is important in the concept of inefficient use of human capital because often it would not be efficient to place these individuals in working opportunities. For this reason, full employment is measured as one hundred percent (100%) employment of individuals in society, not including those that are part of the institutional unemployment.

The inefficient use of human capital that leads to higher unemployment rates is based on a lack of innovation. Until the society reaches the point at which goods and services are provided on an unlimited basis, there is room to grow. This is especially true when there are available resources. Innovation occurs in two forms: developing a way to use existing resources more productively or finding ways to use resources that are not currently being utilized. The lack of innovation fits into the second category. In this way a higher unemployment rate can be seen as a negative, not in the way currently thought, but based on its relation to innovation.

Although not directly related to the strength or weakness of the economy, it is important to analyze the effects of the unemployment rate on both individual workers and employers. The way to analyze the effect is to discuss the overlapping measurement of both workers' and employers' wages.

Wages paid to workers should be viewed as the cost of the resource of human capital. The analysis of how this price is decided is no different than that of any other good or service; it is the product of its supply and demand. If unemployment is high, then there is a high supply of labor relative to the demand for labor. If the supply and demand for labor were equal then all individuals eligible for work would be employed and the unemployment rate would be zero percent (0%).

In our situation, the unemployment rate is above zero percent (0%) and being categorized as "high" which probably indicates it is a large amount above zero. As with other goods and services, the increase in supply in relation to demand decreases prices. In this case, the increase in supply decreases wages. The setup is very similar to the situation of home buying. For example, imagine three employers are offering three different labor-oriented jobs. If there are three employees applying for these jobs, then the third most desirable employee will have equal bargaining power with the third available job. However, if there are six employees applying for those same three jobs, then the last job will have four potential employees. If one of the four employees demands a higher price for his service then one of the other three will simply agree to a lower wage. This same pattern is repeated over the whole market. When there are more people seeking jobs than offering jobs, wages decrease.

A decrease in wages has a negative effect on employees. In the short term prices for goods and services will remain constant or increase with inflation and a decrease or freeze in wages will diminish employees' purchasing power. However, this decrease in wages is a positive for businesses. Lower wages mean lower overall costs and will represent higher profit margins for the business which can lead to many results. The owners of the business may simply pocket the extra money, which will simply be a transfer of wealth from laborers to owners. The lower wages and increase in profit margins could result in more research and development leading to innovation, which has already been shown to improve economic strength. Or, finally, the result of the higher profits could be the hiring of more employees. This result on the market level would shift the balance back towards equality between supply and demand. This shift will continue until the point at which the bargaining power of laborers is greater than that of the employers, resulting in a wage increase. The wage increase will decrease profit margins resulting eventually in the layoff of employees. This layoff will shift the balance back towards higher supply and will start the cycle all over again. It is important to remember that this cycle is constantly occurring within the economy and any high unemployment is just a reflection of the point on the cycle at that given time.

Another result of high unemployment and lower wages is a lower cost passed onto consumers. Labor cost, like the cost of other resources, is an input cost in the production of goods and services. As input costs decrease, producers are able to decrease the price of those goods and services. Clearly this is not always the case as some producers may simply choose to pocket the extra profit. However, in competitive markets in which prices are constantly decreasing down to the point of input costs, the decrease will be translated into lower prices.

For example, Carla is now a successful clothes maker who employs two assistants to help her design and make her clothing. Carla competes with Dave for the clothes business on the island. Both Carla and Dave make high-quality clothes and compete for customers based on their prices. If Carla is able to decrease the wages she pays her employees, she will be able to decrease the price of her clothes. This decrease will allow the island inhabitants to pay lower prices for clothes.

It is important to remember that none of these results equate to the strength or weakness of the economy. Instead these results and effects represent a change in the distribution of wealth. Although important, this does not determine the strength or weakness of the economy as a whole. As discussed earlier, the only measures for strength and weakness are productivity, efficiency, and import surplus. The only element that may be affected by our discussion of employment is efficiency, through increases in innovation based on increased research and development. However, there are more efficient ways than having high unemployment to get to this same increase in innovation and thus it will not be included.

IV. Growing the Pie

At this point in the text it becomes necessary to more fully develop the concept of the economic pie. Earlier in this text the economic pie was used as a way to highlight the difference between economic distribution and economic growth. It is very common for the pie analogy to be used in this context. Changing the distribution of the pie would be the way in which the slices are cut. For instance, imagine there are three children given slices of pie. One child receives one half of the pie while the other two each receive one quarter of the pie. An adult in the room may make the decision that a fairer distribution would be for each child to receive one third of the pie. Economic distribution works in a similar way and can be a policy function addressed by governments.

However, this economic distribution component is completely separate from the economic growth component. Economic strength or weakness is determined by how large the pie is and not how that pie is distributed. Distribution is purely a determination of fairness and is debatable depending on each individual's particular viewpoint. People can differ on whether the person who bakes the pie should get the biggest piece or whether everyone should get the same size piece. However, there can be no disagreement that the bigger the pie the stronger the economic situation.

Again, increasing the size of the pie does not simply mean an increase in GDP. The economic pie is not just made up of the total amount of goods and services within the economy. The goal is to have the most available pie at the lowest possible price. Price in this context is not based on currency but on work. The ultimate goal is to have unlimited amounts of pie with the least amount of baking work possible. There are three ways in which to accomplish this type of pie growth. One, bakers could become more productive by baking more pie in less time. Two, bakers could become more efficient in the use of the resources needed to bake the pie. Three, the bakers could trade a good that takes less time and resources to make for more pies. These are also the three ways in which to grow the economic pie and strengthen the economy. In the following pages these growth methods will be analyzed in more detail. First, however, the premise of the perfect society will be more fully explained. This concept is important for understanding and establishing the way in which the rest of the concepts work together.

The Perfect Society

The basic premise of the rest of this book is based on the perfect society. The perfect society assumes the premise that a society seeks to increase the amount of goods and services available to the individuals living within it. This is the basis of innovation, division of labor, and trade, as discussed in the first section of the book on Economics Island. There is a reason that the individuals on the island did not stick with the original goods and services of berries, clothes, and shelter. The island was better when Alan, Bob, and Carla specialized in the task that they had the competitive advantage in and traded with each other. This allowed them to have the same amount of goods and services, but with less work time. The decrease in work time led to an increase in free time, which has been labeled "leisure time."

The above explanation is crucial in understanding the idea of the perfect society. The island economy was better because the inhabitants had the same amount of goods and services at their disposal but more time to do what they wanted to do. Now a common rebuttal to this idea is that some people like to work and that increased leisure time should not be the goal. However, this argument is missing the point. Leisure time is not an excuse not to work; it is simply an excuse not to *have* to work. Leisure time allows individuals to choose to do with their time what they want, which may or may not include work. It is also important to remember that it is not simply the increase in leisure time but the increase in goods and services that is important. A simple tradeoff between the two is not an improvement in the economy; it is simply a decision on which of the two is more important. Economics Island would also see an economic improvement if the island inhabitants kept their work and leisure time constant but increased the amount of goods and services on the island. For instance, if after the specialization and trading, the inhabitants used their extra time to each catch fish to eat, they would have the same leisure time but an additional good, fish, on the island.

If increasing leisure time and increasing available goods and services is the goal, then it follows that the perfect society would be one in which goods and services were increased to infinity and work time decreased to zero. Cleary this is an impossible point to reach. However, this situation should remain the ideal and all economic growth plans should seek to reach this point. This idea leads to the three methods of increasing economic strength discussed in the following sections of the book.

Productivity

There are only three ways for a society to strengthen its economy: increase productivity, increase efficiency, or increase trade surplus. Productivity is unique in that while efficiency and trade deal with choices based on resources and goods, where to allocate resources and which goods to produce, respectively, productivity deals with labor and production.

Productivity is a function of output and time. *More precisely it is represented by the equation of total output divided by the amount of time needed to reach total output.* In relation to economic strength, the productivity being discussed is labor productivity. Productivity can be measured at many different levels, including individual, company, and societal. Each of these can be demonstrated with an example from the island.

When Alan first began picking berries, he was able to pick one bushel an hour. After one week of picking berries he was able to pick two bushels an hour. In one week Alan had become twice as productive at picking berries. Assume Alan is successful enough as a berry picker, and the demand for his berries is high enough, that he is able to hire a worker to help him pick. Alan is no longer simply an individual picking berries but a berry picking company. He names his new company Alan's Berries. Alan's worker John is not as good as Alan and can only pick one bushel an hour, while Alan is picking two an hour. However, after a week of learning from Alan, John is able to double his productivity and pick two bushels an hour. John doubles his productivity by doubling his output in the same amount of time. However, the company, Alan's Berries, has increased its output from three bushels an hour to four bushels an hour, increasing its productivity by thirty-three percent (33%).

Societal productivity works in the same way. Assume that there are three companies on the island; Alan's Berries, Bob's Shelters, and Carla's Clothes. Each company is able to produce ten of its items a day, bushels of berries, shelters, and articles of clothing, respectively. If Alan's Berries is able to double productivity to twenty bushels while the other two companies keep the same productivity, then society's productivity increases by thirty-three percent (33%) (i.e., from thirty goods a day to forty goods a day). Remember that the increase is based on productivity and not simply output. If Alan is able to double his output by doubling his labor time, then productivity for his company and for society remains the same. There are many ways to increase productivity and some will be described later in this section. However, for now, it is only important to understand these examples as an explanation for how productivity works.

In order to reach the perfect society productivity must be increased. Every society is lacking the perfect society in two ways; it has less than unlimited goods and services and it takes more than zero time in order to produce these goods and services. So, every society can improve by increasing the output of goods and services and decreasing the amount of time it takes to produce these goods and services. An increase in output and decrease in time is an increase in productivity; this can be seen in the equation at the beginning of this section. An increase in economic strength is based on the movement towards the perfect society. This movement, and thus an increase in economic strength, can be achieved by an increase in productivity.

Productivity simply deals with output and time. The way in which the work is performed during that time is not figured into the equation. For instance, it is not any more productive for Alan to sit on a machine that picks the berries for him rather than picking them by hand, if both take the same amount of time and produce the same output. This is based on the idea of leisure time discussed earlier in the book. Alan still has to spend an hour of his time on labor in order to produce one bushel of berries, which takes one hour away from his leisure time. However, this does not mean that the way in which the hour is spent is not important; it is simply not part of the productivity measurement. Instead it is part of the measurement of efficiency. An individual's strength is limited and is a resource just like any other. The way in which this resource is used is part of the efficiency measurement. Alan sitting on a machine and saving his resource of strength may be a more efficient use of the resource than his manual picking. Efficiency will be discussed in the next section. The important point to understand is that productivity is simply a function of output and time.

There are two ways to increase productivity: decrease the amount of time for individual functions of output or decrease the amount of functions needed for output. *Functions of output are simply the steps taken in the production process that lead to output.* For instance, Carla has three functions of output in the production of clothes. First, she must collect the material. Next, she must cut the material to the proper size. Finally, she must tie the material together in order to make the final product. Each of these steps is a function of output. To increase productivity Carla could either decrease the time one or more of these steps take, while holding the others constant, or remove one of these steps from the process. For example, assume that each step takes Carla three hours to complete for a total labor time of nine hours. If

Carla were able to decrease the time it took to complete each task to two hours, she would increase her productivity by fifty percent (50%). Similarly, if she were able to remove one of the steps to go from three steps to two, her productivity would similarly increase by fifty percent (50%).

A decrease in the time it takes to perform a function of output can be brought about in three ways: knowledge, incentive, and replacement. Functions of output are performed by individuals. In some functions individuals are aided by non-human sources, computers, machinery, etc., however each function requires some human element at some point along the process. Knowledge refers to the individual's effectiveness in performing a particular function of output. Individuals have a baseline of knowledge for every function they perform. If they did not have this basic knowledge they would not be able to perform the task. An improvement in this basic knowledge can lead to a decrease in the amount of time it takes to perform the function.

For example, when Alan first began picking berries his knowledge base was simply the act of plucking berries from the bushes and bringing them over to place in a pile on the sand. As time went on Alan learned that if he picked the berries by moving down each row instead of picking the berries at random, he would save time. He also learned that if he waited until his hands were full to place the berries on the sand, he would make fewer trips away from picking which would save time. These two changes in strategy represent increases in knowledge related to the function of picking berries. The increase in knowledge led to a decrease in the time it took to perform the function, while output, the amount of berries picked, remained constant. This represents an increase in productivity through an increase in knowledge.

An increase in incentive for workers can also increase productivity. Workers complete tasks based on both their knowledge of the task as well as their willingness to complete the task. For example, Alan may have the knowledge to pick berries at a productive rate, but he may simply choose to pick the berries in a less productive way. Now because Alan is picking berries for either his own consumption or for trade with other inhabitants it can be assumed that he does not need an incentive to be productive.

However, if Alan paid John to help him pick berries at an hourly rate, John may not have an incentive to work as productively as he can. His incentive may simply be the fear of being fired, which may require him to rise above a certain minimum productivity level and no more. It is not only workers compensated on an hourly basis who may lack incentive. Without delving too much into governmental affairs, it should be noted that policy can have a big effect on incentive. For instance, if Alan is required to provide half of every bushel after the tenth bushel he picks to the government, then it may not be worth it to him to try to increase his productivity. If he is able to pick ten bushels comfortably, it may not be worth it for him to try to increase his knowledge base or implement the changes from his increase in knowledge if half the additional bushels picked cannot be consumed or traded by Alan. The ways in which incentives are increased or decreased based on governmental policy is too lengthy a discussion for this text; it is only necessary to understand that productivity can be affected by incentives.

The final way to increase productivity is through replacement. The replacement is of individual laborers with non-human labor. This replacement often comes in the form of technological advance. What is important is that work that was previously being completed by an individual or a group of individuals is now being completed by some form of non-human labor. Again, a distinction must be made here between the replacement of labor and the difficulty of labor. This can better be shown through an example from the island. Imagine Alan develops a machine that he can sit on while it picks up the berries for him. The machine picks berries up at the same rate as Alan, so although the work is less physically demanding, it still takes him the same amount of time to pick the berries. The work may be physically easier, as he no longer has to bend down to pick up the berries, but he still loses the same amount of time sitting on the machine and thus no replacement has taken place. His productivity has not increased at all with the machine. However, imagine that Alan develops a machine in which all he needs to do is press a button and the machine is able to pick all the berries needed. Alan does not need to stay and watch the machine but is free to do whatever he wants while the berries are being picked. Now, Alan is being replaced by the machine. He is still necessary to turn on the machine, etc., but much less time is spent. This replacement of part of a function of production decreases the individual's labor time and thus increases productivity.

The other way to increase productivity is to remove steps from the process of functions of production. The easiest way to explain this concept is with a similar example from the island. Above, the example of Carla's clothes making was used to show the effects of removing one of the three steps in this process, mainly the increase in productivity by fifty percent (50%). Removing steps from the process of functions of production is similar to decreasing the time for these processes. The same three concepts, knowledge, incentive, and replacement, can be utilized in the removal of steps. The concept of incentive is the same in both examples. Individuals can perform as many or as few steps as they choose based on their incentive levels.

Knowledge and replacement also work in a similar way in removing steps and in decreasing the time it takes to perform steps. Here another example from the island is useful. Alan can remove a step from his berry picking process by utilizing knowledge and replacement in one invention. Alan had been collecting only as many berries as he could hold in his hands and then bringing them to the sand. This required him to make twenty trips from the berry bushes to the sand to collect the berries. After a while Alan realized that if he could develop a way to hold more berries at one time he could decrease the amount of trips he would have to make outside the bushes, which would save him time. So, he developed a sack that could hold enough berries that he would only have to walk to the sand one time at the end of all his picking. In this way, he used an increase in knowledge to develop the sack which replaced his function. The replacement occurred because what normally took Alan added work time, the multiple trips from and back to the bushes, was replaced by the extra capacity of the sack. These multiple trips were each a step taken in the process of collecting berries. The removal of these steps decreases the total time for the function of production. It is important that along with the removal of a step, there is not an accompanied increase in the time the other steps take. The assumption is that the time it takes to complete the other steps that are not removed remains constant or, at the very least, the increase in the time of the other steps is less than the time saved by the removal of the step. Also, the output cannot be affected by the removal of the step. These concepts are keeping consistent with the definition of productivity as total output divided by the total time it takes for that output.

The fundamental concepts to take away are that the two ways to increase productivity are to decrease the time it takes for one or more steps in the function of production or to remove one or more of the steps, without decreasing output. The three ways to accomplish the decrease in time or removal of steps are knowledge, incentive, and replacement. Increasing productivity is important because along with efficiency and trade surplus it is the only way to grow the economic pie and increase economic strength.

Efficiency

Efficiency is an extremely important concept in economic thinking and the second way in which an economy can be strengthened. The significance of efficiency can be seen in the definition of economics mentioned in the first section: *the study of the most efficient use of scarce goods*. A good can be used in many different ways for many different purposes. In this discussion, goods will mean those used for production. These goods are called intermediate goods because they are used in conjunction with others in the production of final goods. So, intermediate goods are used for production while final goods are sold in the market to customers. Efficiency can also be discussed in terms of resources, which like intermediate goods, are used in the production of other goods.

Although resources or intermediate goods can be used to produce many different goods, all uses are not created equal. Some uses will yield better production than others. Better is not a subjective determination based on likes and dislikes, but instead a quantitative measurement of comparative goods. For instance, if we assume that a bushel of berries is equal to the value of one piece of clothing, then two bushels of berries can be determined to be a better production than a piece of clothing. Thus if the same resource, or intermediate good, can be used for one of two purposes, collecting two bushels of berries or creating a piece of clothing, then the resource or intermediate good's more efficient use would be in collecting two bushels of berries. This example is expanded below to help illustrate the point.

On the island there are many palm trees with coconuts growing on them. These coconuts can be used as resources, intermediate goods, or final goods. As a resource, the whole coconut or part of the coconut would be used in production. As an intermediate good the coconut would be produced into a good that would then be used in turn for final production. An example, and the one that will be used to illustrate efficiency, is if the coconut shell is hollowed out and used as a bucket. Now this bucket could be considered a final good, but because it is going to be used to help produce the output of berries, it will be described as an intermediate good in this example. As a final good the coconut would be sold or bartered on the market in its original form. The differences are not important except to highlight that the measure of efficiency is not determinant on which form the good is in, only its effect on output.

The first to discover the coconuts on the island is Alan. After taking the coconut off the tree Alan discovers that if he cuts it open he can use it to chop the berries off the bush instead of picking them with his hand. In doing this he is able to limit the time it takes him to pick the berries because each swipe of the coconut shell takes three berries off the bush as opposed to only one when his hand alone is used. Since he is able to hold onto six berries at a time before he has to bring them over to the area where he keeps them, it cuts down the amount of arm swipes during each trip from six to two.

After a while Alan notices the curved shape of the coconut and realizes that it may be able to hold and transport the berries. Instead of having to walk over to the designated area each time he picks six berries, he would be able to pick all needed berries, place them in the coconut, and then walk them all over to the designated area. This would save time by cutting down that amount of walking time. Now with the amount of coconuts on the island Alan is able to use one to help pick the berries and one to help transport the berries. But imagine if there was only one coconut on the island and Alan had to decide in which way to use that one coconut. At this point it is useful and necessary, if not a little tedious, to quantify the help given by each of the uses of the coconut.

It takes Alan one minute to pick six berries and one minute to walk the berries over to their designated area. He needs to collect sixty berries total, which takes twenty minutes; ten minutes for picking and ten minutes for walking. If the coconut is used for picking it will decrease the time for picking down to three minutes and twenty seconds (one third of ten minutes). However, Alan will still need to walk over to the designated area ten times which will still take ten minutes. This will make his total picking and walking time thirteen minutes and twenty seconds. If the coconut is used as a bucket then it will still take ten minutes to pick, but only one minute to walk over to the designated area. This is because only one trip with the berries will be needed. So, if the coconut is used as a bucket it decreases the total picking and walking time to eleven minutes. Using the coconut as a bucket instead of a picker saves more time for Alan and is therefore more efficient. If it can only be used for one of the two intermediate goods it is more efficient to use it as a bucket.

It is important to emphasize that efficiency can mean both higher productivity, as seen in the example above, or less usage. Using the coconut as a bucket results in less labor time for Alan than using it as a picker. In this way, the most efficient use for the coconut is as a bucket because it saves the most time. However, the example could be reworked so that the labor time required is the same no matter how the coconut is used, but that it takes fewer coconuts when used as a bucket. For instance, if using two coconuts to pick takes the same amount of time as using one coconut as a bucket then the use as a bucket is still more efficient. It no longer is more productive, as the amount of labor time required is the same, but less of the scarce resource of coconuts is used which makes it more efficient.

As mentioned earlier in the book, resources are scarce, simply meaning that there is a finite supply. Thus, it is important to minimize the use of these resources when possible. The perfect society is impossible partly because of the scarcity of resources. No matter how productive or efficient society becomes, it will always require some resource or a portion of a resource to create goods. In order to get to the perfect society, infinite goods are necessary and thus infinite resources as well. Whether using less of the scarce resources or increasing productivity, increasing efficiency brings us closer to the perfect society. Increasing efficiency increases the output of goods and services while decreasing the amount of resources, including workers' time and energy. Using this analysis it is easy to see how increasing efficiency over the entire economy is the second way in which the economic pie can be grown.

Again, the perfect society represents an infinite economic pie; the pie being the amount of goods and services available in the society discounted by the amount of people using these goods and services. How the pie is divided is not a concern in this analysis, only the total size of the pie. The pie will never be infinite because the perfect society will never exist. But the closer you get to the perfect society the larger the pie grows.

Trade Surplus

The third way in which to grow the economic pie is by increasing trade surplus. *Trade Surplus is the difference between the total amount of resources, time, and energy used in the production of exports and the total amount of resources, time, and energy that would be needed to create imports.* A trade surplus exists when the figure for imports is higher than that of exports. The calculation is interesting because it is comparing the actual input costs (resources, time, and energy) for exports and the saved input costs for imports. The imports have their own actual input costs; however, these costs are borne by the country or area of their production and thus are not important in the calculation for growing our economic pie. What is important for us, is the amount of input costs that would be required if we were to produce those same imports in our economy. When trade occurs, if the trade surplus is positive it means that the economy is saving resources, time, and energy that would be required if those goods were not traded for but produced in our economy. The larger the trade surplus, the closer the economy is moving towards the perfect society and the bigger the economic pie is growing.

It is important to understand that the trade surplus being discussed in this section has nothing to do with the terms "trade surplus and deficit" that are commonly discussed in economic analysis. When the surplus and deficit of trade are discussed normally, it is in terms of net exports less net imports. It is a measure of the value of the goods we are sending out of the country compared to the value of the goods being brought in. A country with a large trade surplus exports more goods than it imports, or is a net exporter. In this measure, exporting is seen as good because it means that there is a large market and a high demand for goods and services produced within the country. Also, it means that imports are low, relatively, compared with exports, meaning that we are able to satisfy demand from goods produced within the country and don't need to bring them in from other countries. However, this measure does not take into account any of the input costs associated with the production of the goods. For this reason, it is important to differentiate between the common meaning of trade surplus and the meaning which it takes in this text.

Trade surplus is a different type of measure than either productivity or efficiency because it is affected by external factors outside of the economy. Productivity and efficiency are entirely contained within our economy and based on the ways production is performed. Trade surplus, although it may be affected by both productivity and efficiency, is based on the choices made about what goods and services are produced.

An economy with a high trade surplus is consuming less resources, time, and energy but having access to more goods and services. Again, this principle needs to be looked at in terms of the perfect society. If the ideal is to get the maximum amount of goods and services with the least amount of work then the higher the trade surplus the closer to the perfect society. A situation in which the trade surplus would be at its maximum is if the economy was able to import all of the goods and services produced outside of its region without needing to export any of the goods it produced within its region. This is obviously impossible because the other economies are rational actors and would not trade something for nothing. *Rational actors being defined as individuals (or in this case whole economies) that make decisions based on rational expectations without the interference of subjective or emotional determinations.* However, the closer a society can get to this situation the better. In other words, economies should seek to minimize the amount of exports needed to maximize the amount of imports they receive.

The minimization of exports and maximization of imports do not refer to simply the quantitative, but also the qualitative nature of the goods and services. This is because the economy is trying to limit resources, time, and energy. For instance, exporting ten berries would be better than five articles of clothing, because the time and energy required to get berries is far less than what is required to make an article of clothing. This is also true in reverse as it applies to imports. Importing five articles of clothing is better than ten berries because of the time and energy saved. If the economy can import the articles of clothing then it does not need to produce them. Not having to produce the clothing is better than not having to produce the berries because it allows more time and energy to be used for other goods and services. A more extended illustration from the island may provide a better explanation.

For this example, the island will be joined by two other economies: mainland and peninsula. Mainland is a new economy that has not yet developed to the extent of the island. Mainland consists mostly of individuals collecting their own food and shelter. No one has been able to make any clothing and the only good that is mass produced is the berries that are abundant on the mainland. The peninsula is a little more advanced; they have begun to have a division of labor. The good that the peninsula is able to mass produce is the buckets made of hollowed-out coconuts. The island is the most developed and has many goods and services. The good that is most desired by both the mainland and the peninsula is clothing.

The mainland trades the berries it collects for the coconut buckets produced on the peninsula. The collection of berries is relatively universal, in relation to time and energy, among the island, mainland, and peninsula. This is because the process is the same in all three economies and there is not much room for technological or innovative advance. This is important when thinking about trade surplus. To collect a bushel of berries takes one hour. The mainland trades five bushels of berries for each coconut bucket. This is because the coconut buckets are useful to the mainland but the individuals there do not know how to produce them. To them, one bucket is worth five bushels of berries. In the long run each bucket cuts down the amount of time it takes to collect a bushel of berries by six so it is worth five bushels. For the peninsula, it only takes two hours to produce the coconut buckets. In return they get five bushels of berries that would take five hours to produce.

The peninsula is saving three hours of labor for each trade they make, which gives them a trade surplus.

The island, being the most advanced and innovative of the economies, is able to produce clothing that neither the mainland nor the peninsula can create. This clothing is highly desired by the mainland and the peninsula. The mainland is still only able to trade berries. However, because they desire the clothing more than the peninsula and have no ability to make the clothes, they are willing to trade fifteen bushels of berries for each piece of clothing. As stated before, the collection of berries is universal, in terms of time and energy, across the three economies. It takes the island the same one hour per bushel of berries that it takes both the peninsula and the mainland. The fifteen bushels that the island receives in their trade with the mainland decreases their total amount of work hours by fifteen hours. The item that is traded for these fifteen bushels is one piece of clothing. This piece of clothing only takes the island five hours to make. The total net work saved (hours for a piece of clothing less hours saved from not having to produce fifteen bushels of berries) is ten hours. This creates a trade surplus for the island economy.

It is important to look at what the increase in trade surplus means for each economy. The measure for trade surplus used here is different than the measure of trade surplus and deficit commonly used. The commonly used meaning creates a zero sum situation. This means that for each increase in the trade surplus of one nation there must be a similar decrease in the trade surplus (or increase in trade deficit) of another nation. This is because the measure is based on quantity, and if the quantity of imports goes up in one country it means that the quantity of exports has gone up in another country. However, in the measure of trade surplus used here every economy can have a trade surplus. In fact, based on the reasons for trading explained in the first section of the text, every nation *should* have a surplus. The reason for trade is to minimize the amount of time and energy required for the production of goods. And because of specialization, most trades allow a nation to decrease the time and energy used compared to producing all goods and services themselves. Thus, it is not whether there is a trade surplus or not, but how large this surplus is in relation to previous surpluses. As an economy grows this trade surplus grows with the economy as a whole.

It is difficult for the modern reader to reconcile the principles listed above with the current economic scenario of today, one in which there has been an evolution from a barter society to one that relies on a fixed monetary unit for exchange. That is to say, that imports and exports are not traded in a good for good form but in a buy and sell form. When the United States imports computers from Japan it does not offer in exchange a package of apple pies. The U.S. buys computers with money and it sells its apple pies for money. This is where the understanding of money simply as a tool to make trading more manageable is important. This point needs to be understood because it leads to the comprehension that the buying and selling of goods with a monetary unit is, at its core, a trade of goods. The means by which the sale is made is different, but the end is the same. In a given period, goods are imported and goods are exported from a given economy and whether these goods are paid for in dollars, yen, or notes it still results in the same calculation: goods imported less goods exported.

On the island, the monetary units used for exchange are palm leaves. Instead of trading a piece of clothing for fifteen bushels of berries, the island purchases the berries with palm leaves. A piece of clothing costs five palm leaves while every three bushels of berries costs one palm leaf. So, each piece of clothing costs the same amount as fifteen bushels of berries. However, over time, the mainland develops a way to make clothing. The mainland still desires clothing from the island, but it is now worth less to them, because if needed they can make the clothing themselves. If they were still trading then they would simply offer fewer bushels of berries, maybe ten, in exchange for each piece of clothing. However, this would be a time-consuming exercise and would need to be replicated many times over. Working with the monetary exchange tool of palm leaves, the island, observing the decreasing demand, simply lowers the price of clothing to three leaves. The island is now exporting the same amount of clothes to the mainland, but is receiving less palm leaves. When the island attempts to purchase goods from other economies it will have less palm leaves to use, which will result in less imports. The island, in this way, is like an individual; the less monetary units it has, in this case palm leaves, the less goods it will be able to purchase. For the island this means a decrease in imports.

The last point to make is that monetary units are valued simply on the value of the goods they can be exchanged for. In this case the palm leaf on its own is worthless but its ability to be exchanged for berries, buckets, and clothing gives it worth. Like goods and services, monetary units can gain or lose value based on supply and demand. However, this does not contradict the earlier point. This supply and demand is based on the units' ability to be exchanged, not the units' own intrinsic value.

The island has fifty palm leaves that are used for exchange both on the island, and between it, the mainland, and peninsula. The island has all fifty palm leaves and the other economies don't have any. The island then uses those fifty palm leaves to purchase one hundred and fifty bushels of berries from the mainland. (This exchange is still based on fifteen bushels of berries for each piece of clothing, which makes each bushel one-third of a palm leaf and each piece of clothing five palm leaves). Now, the mainland has all fifty palm leaves. In turn, the mainland could use those fifty palm leaves to purchase ten pieces of clothing. This would work out to fifteen bushels of berries received for every one piece of clothing sent out, which is the proper exchange. However, if suddenly, while the fifty palm leaves were held on the mainland, fifty more palm leaves were added into the economy then the mainland would hold one hundred palm leaves. If they attempted to exchange these palm leaves for clothing, they would receive twenty pieces of clothing. This would mean that they had received one piece of clothing for every seven and a half bushels of berries. But, the values of the underlying goods, berries and clothes, did not go up or down. The supply and demand of the goods stayed constant, only the monetary exchange tool changed. For this reason, along with the supply and demand considerations addressed in the first section, the purchasing power of the palm leaf would decrease in half, meaning that each piece of clothing would now cost ten palms instead of five.

The other cause for the purchasing power of monetary units of exchange to decrease is when the demand for the unit itself decreases. The most common reason for this decrease in demand is lack of confidence in the monetary unit. If the units are only as valuable as the goods and services they can be exchanged for, then a loss in confidence in their ability to be exchanged would make them less valuable. The loss of confidence could happen for various reasons. Individuals could be nervous that the supply of the unit would go up, making the units less valuable, or simply that good and service providers could stop accepting the units as an exchange. In these cases, individuals would not want to be stuck holding these units when this loss of confidence occurs, so they will demand more of them in exchange for the goods and services to offset the risk. It will take more units of exchange to purchase the same good or service based on the decrease in demand for that unit.

The most common examples of a decrease in the inherent value of monetary units of exchange occur in the currency of crisis-stricken countries. A civil war, disease outbreak, or instability in the ruling government can cause a country's currency to be viewed with unease and nervousness by outsiders. Individuals, businesses, and other countries will be scared of being stuck holding the currency as it loses value. This will cause these individuals, businesses, and countries to unload the currency at a discount causing the currency to lose value.

The above information adds another dimension to the trade surplus analysis. An economy can grow by increasing the value of its goods and services vis-a-vis other economies but also by increasing the value of its monetary units of exchange vis-a-vis other economies. The same analysis that was done using goods from the island and goods from the mainland can be used with goods from the mainland and palm leaves from the island. Instead of trading clothes for berries, the island purchases berries with palm leaves. If the amount of palm leaves needed to purchase a bushel of berries decreases from five to four, then the island has grown its economy by increasing its trade surplus.

Trade surplus is the difference between the value, calculated in terms of time and energy used in production, of an economy's imports and exports. The higher the trade surplus, meaning the value of imports is higher than exports, the more the economy grows. Trade surplus is the third and final way an economy can grow, along with productivity and efficiency. An economy increases its trade surplus through the choices it makes on what goods and services to produce along with its ability to keep the value of its monetary units of exchange high.

An economy should produce those goods and services that are sought most highly by other economies and thus able to be exchanged for the highest value. An economy can keep the value of its monetary unit of exchange high by limiting supply and maximizing demand. Demand is maximized by limiting or preferably eliminating loss of confidence in the unit. Taking these steps will increase trade surplus and grow the economy.

V. Conclusion

Hopefully, the examples of Economics Island have been informative in the understanding of basic economic principles. The progression from individual producer/consumer to bartering through comparative advantage to exchanges using monetary units mimics the path that economies have taken over time. It has not been as neat or linear as our examples on Economics Island, but has occurred all the same. This progression gives insight into the workings of the present more complex economic structures of today. Understanding that the purchase of a good or service with a monetary unit of exchange is no different than a trade of two goods helps to illustrate the fundamental nature of the current economy.

Once these basic foundational ideas of the economy are expressed, the goal of the economy can be determined. The perfect society is one in which all goods and services are unlimited and require no work to produce. This society is obviously impossible, however, each economy can seek to move as close to this society as possible. Here is where the notion of "growing the pie" derives. The pie is the total goods and services within the economy, either produced or obtained through trade. The goal is to increase the amount of theses goods and services while decreasing the amount of input time, energy, and resources required for production. In this analysis it does not matter how these goods and services are distributed once they are in the economy, only that the economy has them. The more the pie grows, the closer to the perfect society the economy becomes.

The economy grows in three ways: through increased production, increased efficiency, and through an increase in the trade surplus. Productivity is derived by the equation of total output divided by the amount of time needed to reach total output. Productivity is increased in two ways; decreasing the amount of functions needed in production or decreasing the amount of time it takes to perform the individual functions. An economy can increase productivity either by creating new ways to perform the functions of production or by increasing the incentive for speed in production. The first depends on the innovation in techniques and tools while the latter is based on the feelings of the individual worker. Utilizing either of these methods leads to increased productivity which leads to growth in the economy.

The second way to grow the economy is through increased efficiency. Efficiency deals with the amount of resources needed for output. The fewer resources used, the more efficient the production. This efficiency includes natural resources as well human capital in the form of time and energy. Efficiency matters because resources are not infinite. This is why economics is said to be the study of the allocation of scarce resources. The scarcity of resources is one of the reasons that the perfect society is impossible. However, economies can seek to use the least amount of resources possible in the production of goods and services which will move them closer to the perfect society. Efficiency can be increased by using resources for the purposes that create the most production with the least use. This is a decision-making process as to what the best use of each resource will be, depending on its production output. These resources also include the time and energy of human output, so that this decision-making process also applies to the ways individuals decide to use their time and energy in production. Increased efficiency, like increased production, will grow the economy and move it closer to the perfect society.

The final way to grow the economy is through an increase in the trade surplus. The trade surplus used here is different than what is commonly referred to as trade surplus and trade deficit in economics. An economy's trade surplus, as described in the text for purposes of this analysis, is calculated as the input costs of total imports less the input costs of total exports. The input costs described refer to all resources, time, and energy used in the production of the goods and services being imported and exported. The goal in moving towards the perfect society is to have the most total amount of goods and services with the least amount of work. If your surplus is high, meaning the input costs of imports are higher than the input costs of exports, then the economy has decreased input costs through the trade. In the perfect society, input costs are zero so every trade that decreases input costs moves an economy closer to the perfect society. In this way, just as with increasing productivity and efficiency, increasing trade surplus grows the economy.

The economy is extremely important to most people's everyday lives. It affects individuals' budgets, jobs, and most everyday decisions. The study of economics is complex and far-reaching. Many experts, smarter than this author, have spent entire careers studying and modeling how and why the economy works the way it does. The first goal of this text was to outline the basic concepts involved in the operation of the economy in a way that was hopefully accessible to all readers, not just those with an economics degree. It is the author's hope that this was accomplished through the use of the island as an illustrative tool. The second goal was to explore the way in which to grow the economy. Specifically, by increasing productivity, efficiency, and trade surplus. In this section it was important to describe why the current measures used to determine the growth of the economy are not accurate. Also, an exploration of, what in this text has been called, the perfect society has been made as a way to show why increasing productivity, efficiency, and trade surplus is the only way to grow the economy.

Hopefully the two goals outlined above were achieved in the text and the reader has come away with a better understanding of the economy. It is important to understand the evolution of the economic structure in order to understand the current complex economic system. This is why the educational illustration of the island was used. In conclusion, I hope lessons were learned from economics island, most importantly, how to grow the economy.